This
Coloring Book Belongs To

Color Test Pages

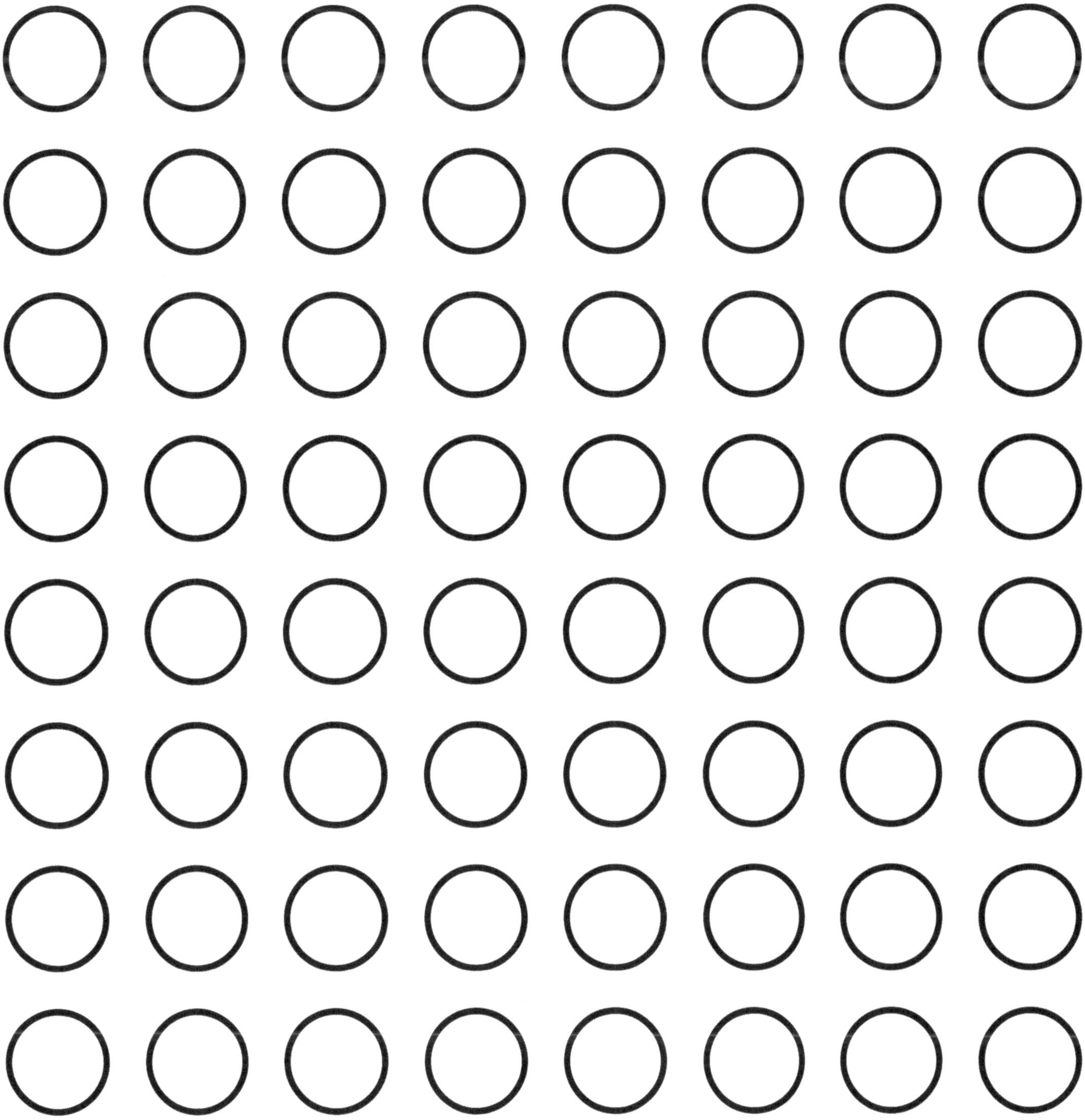

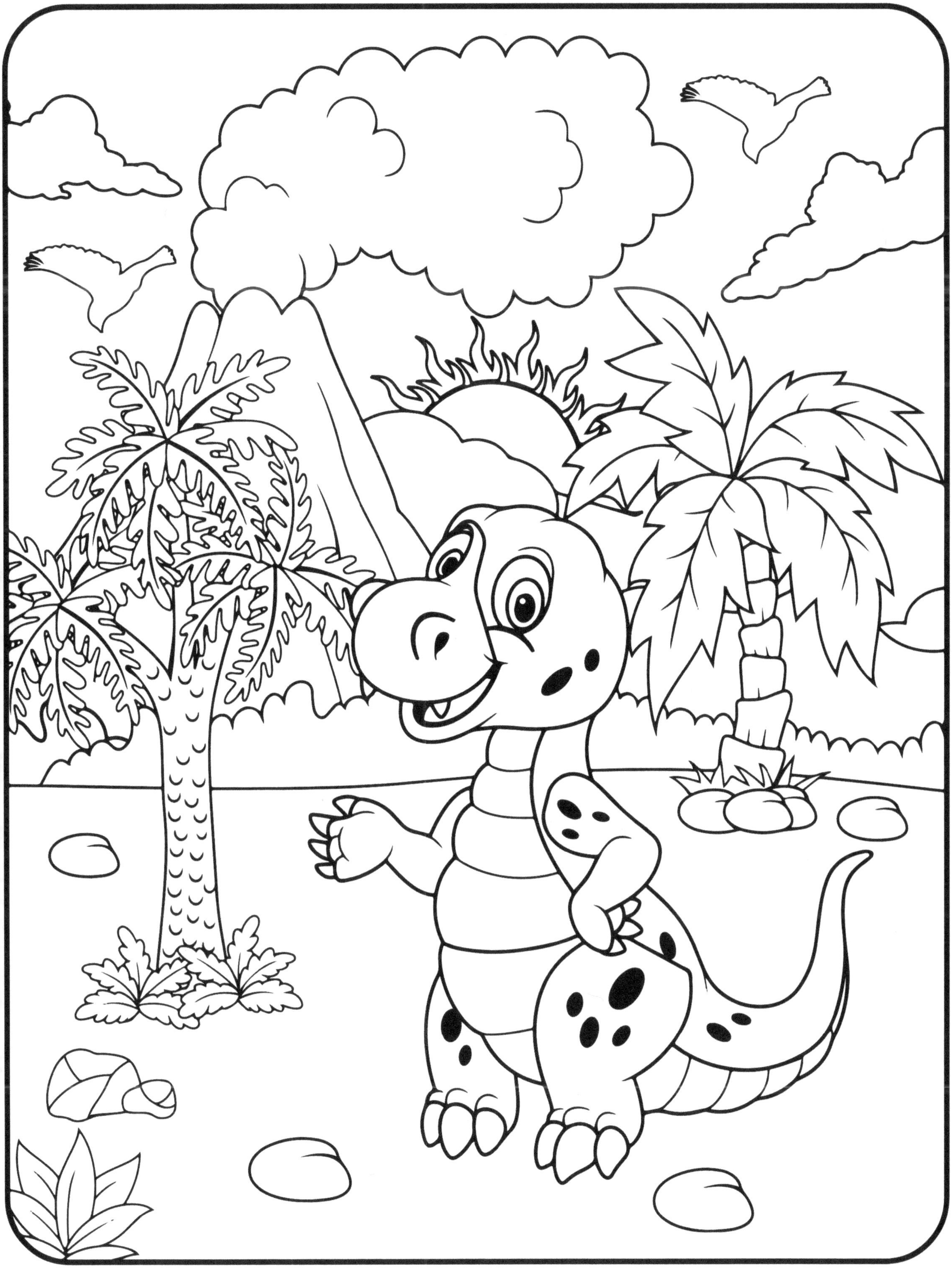

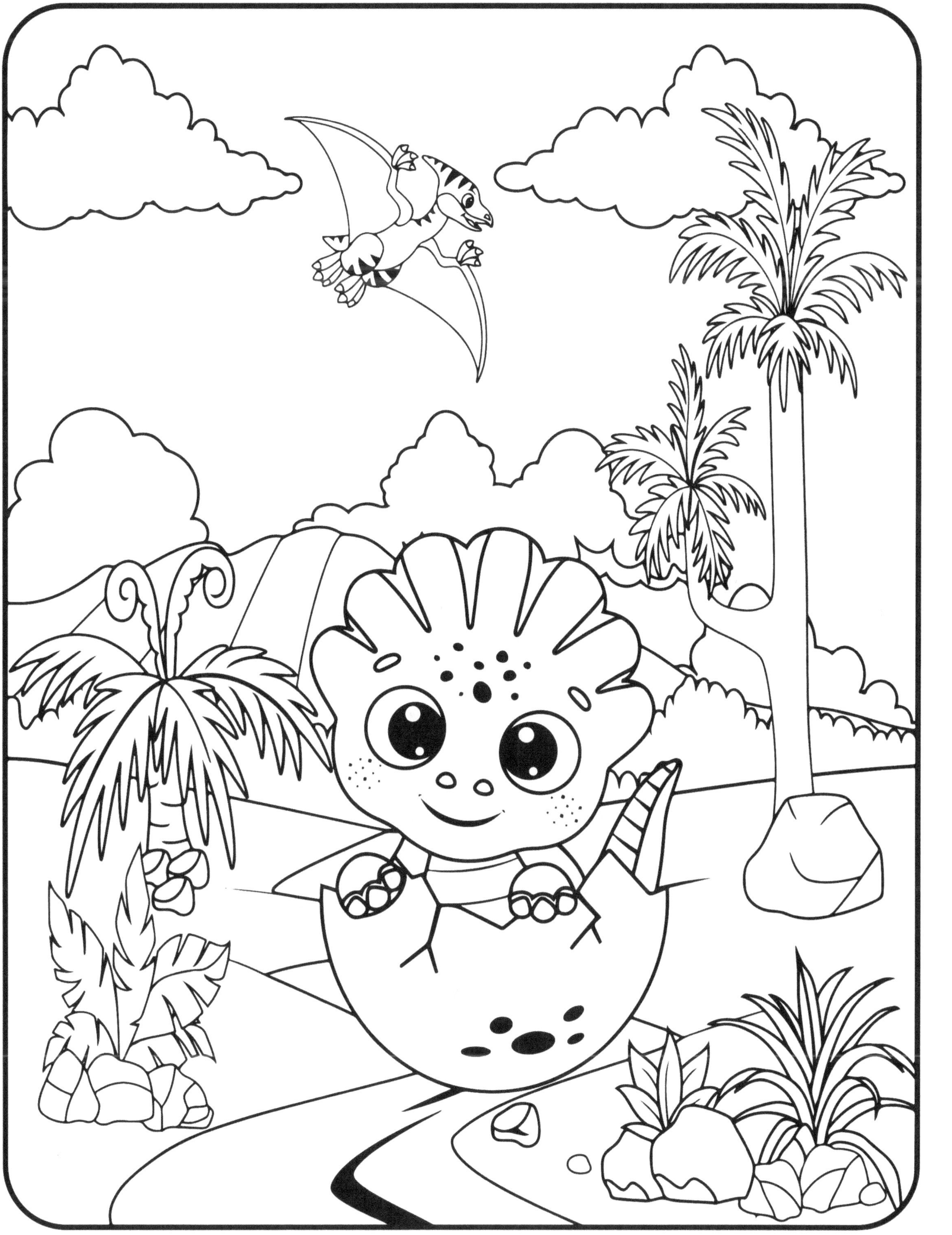

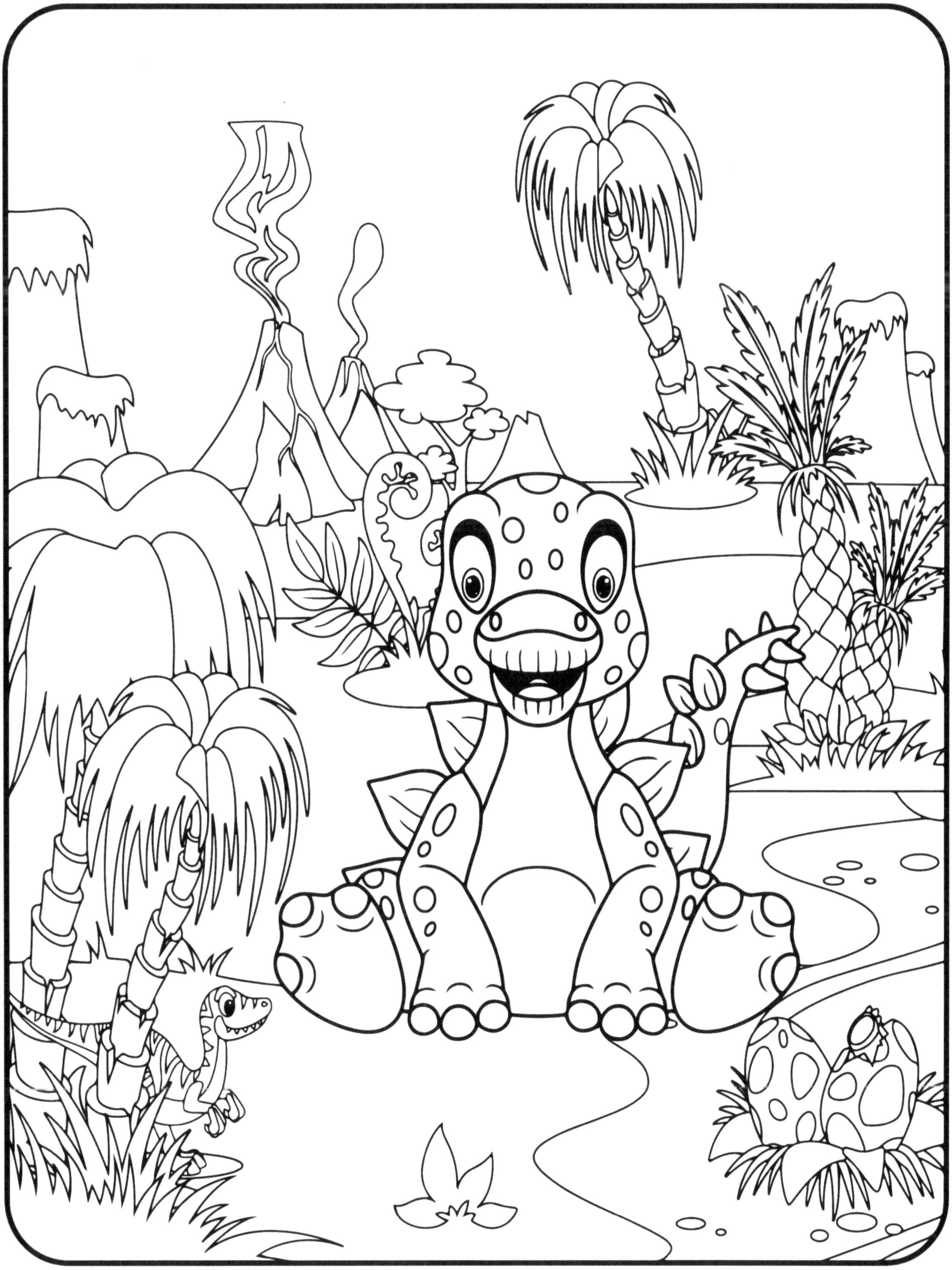

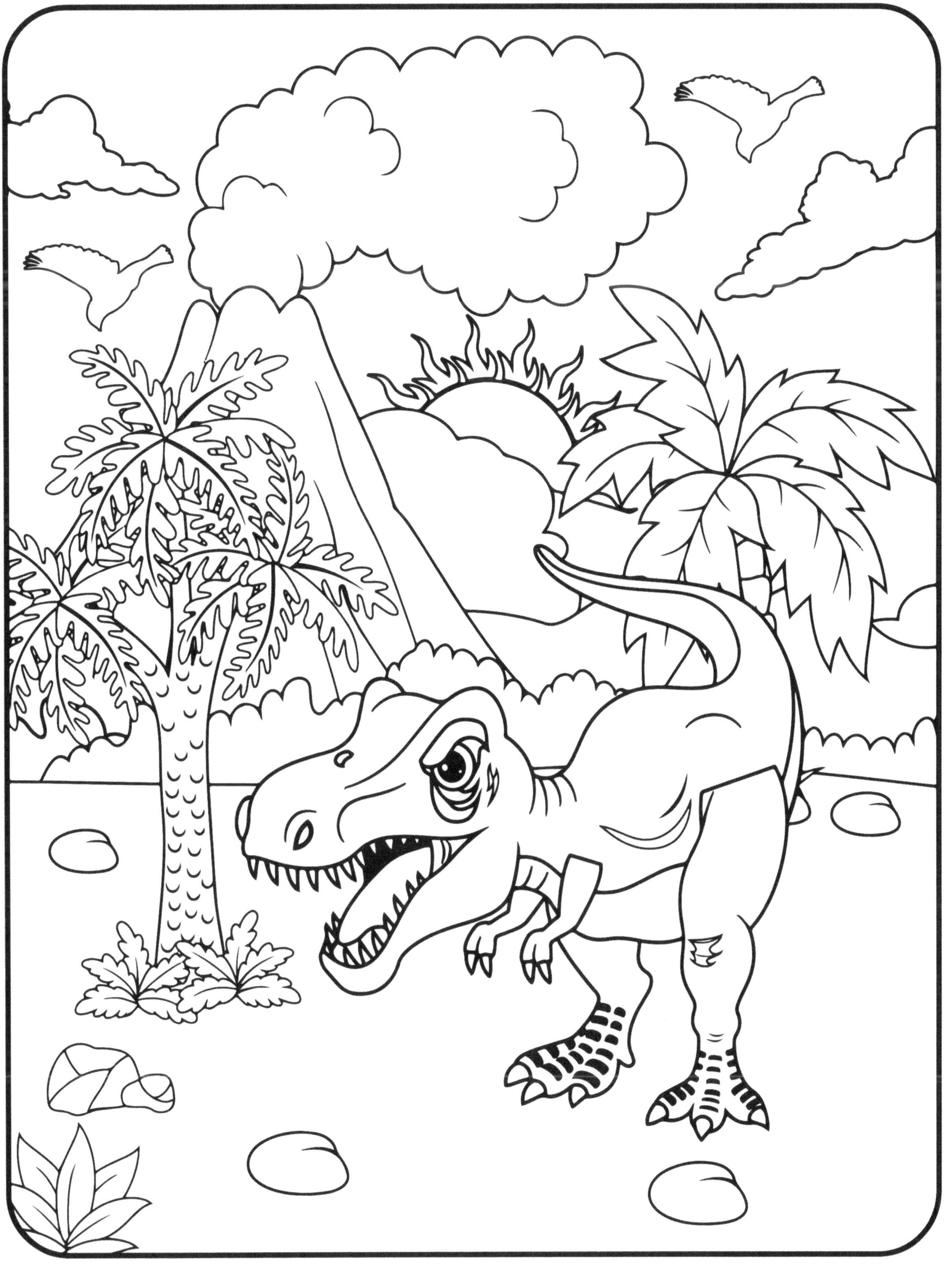

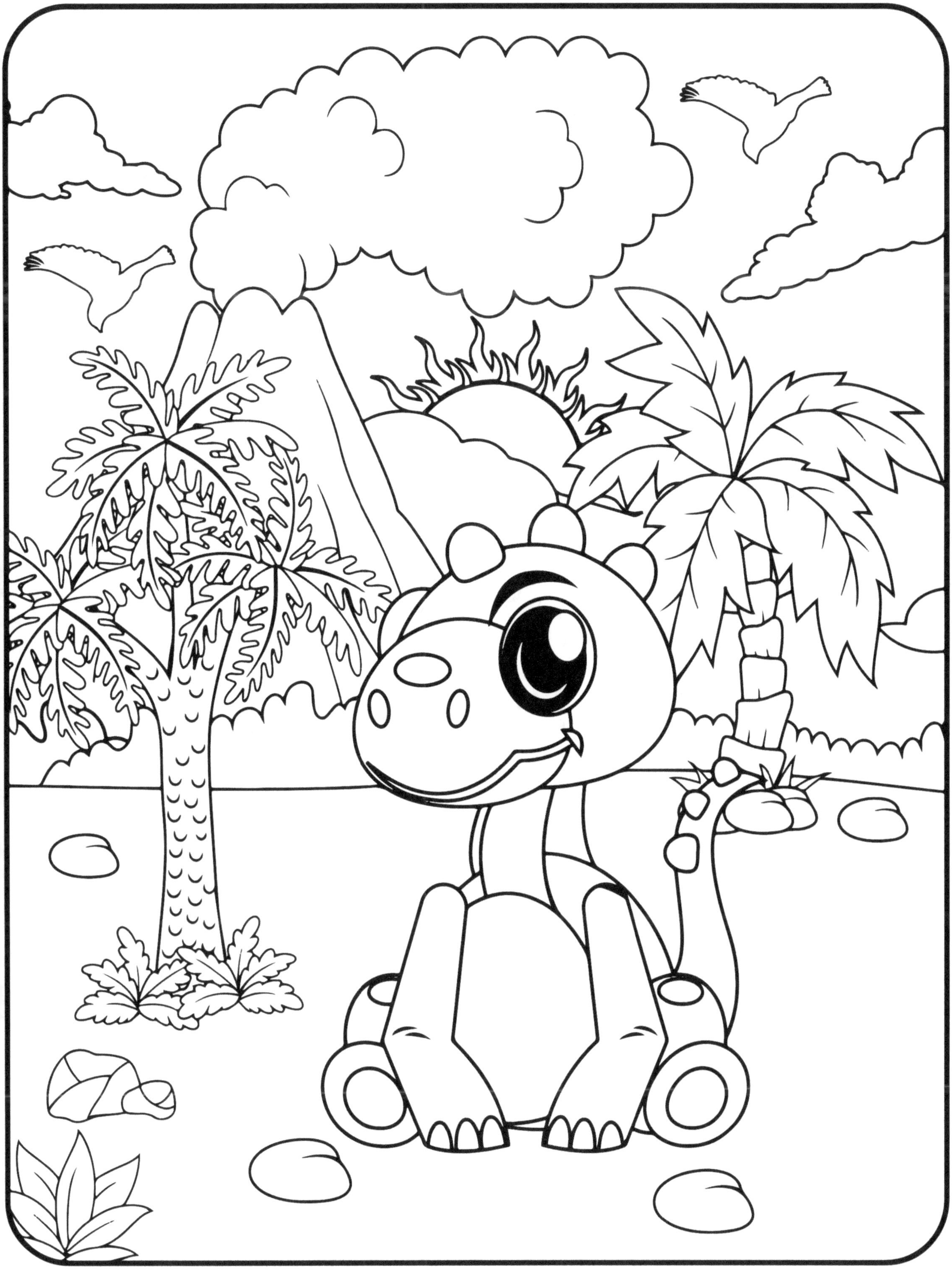

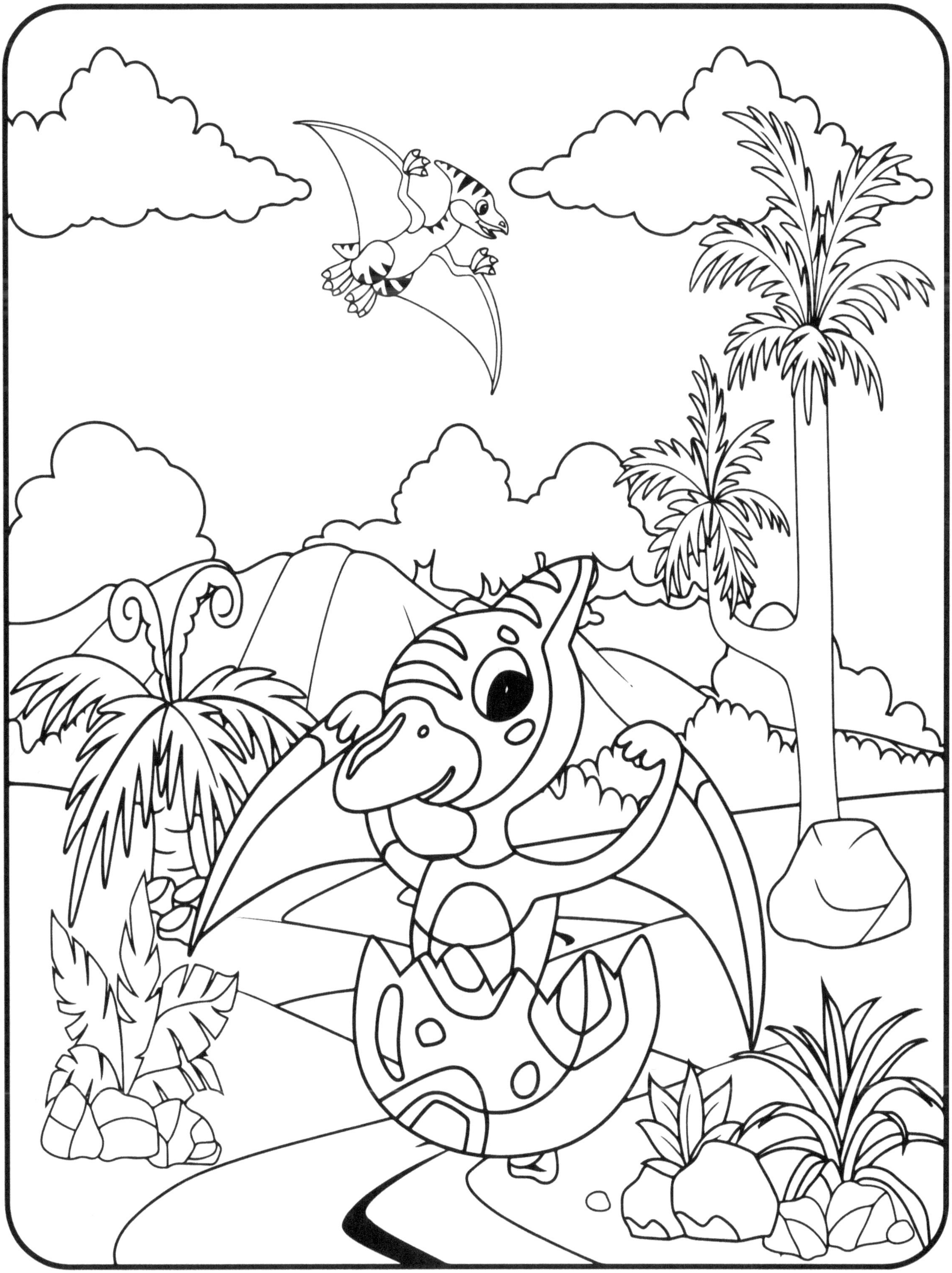

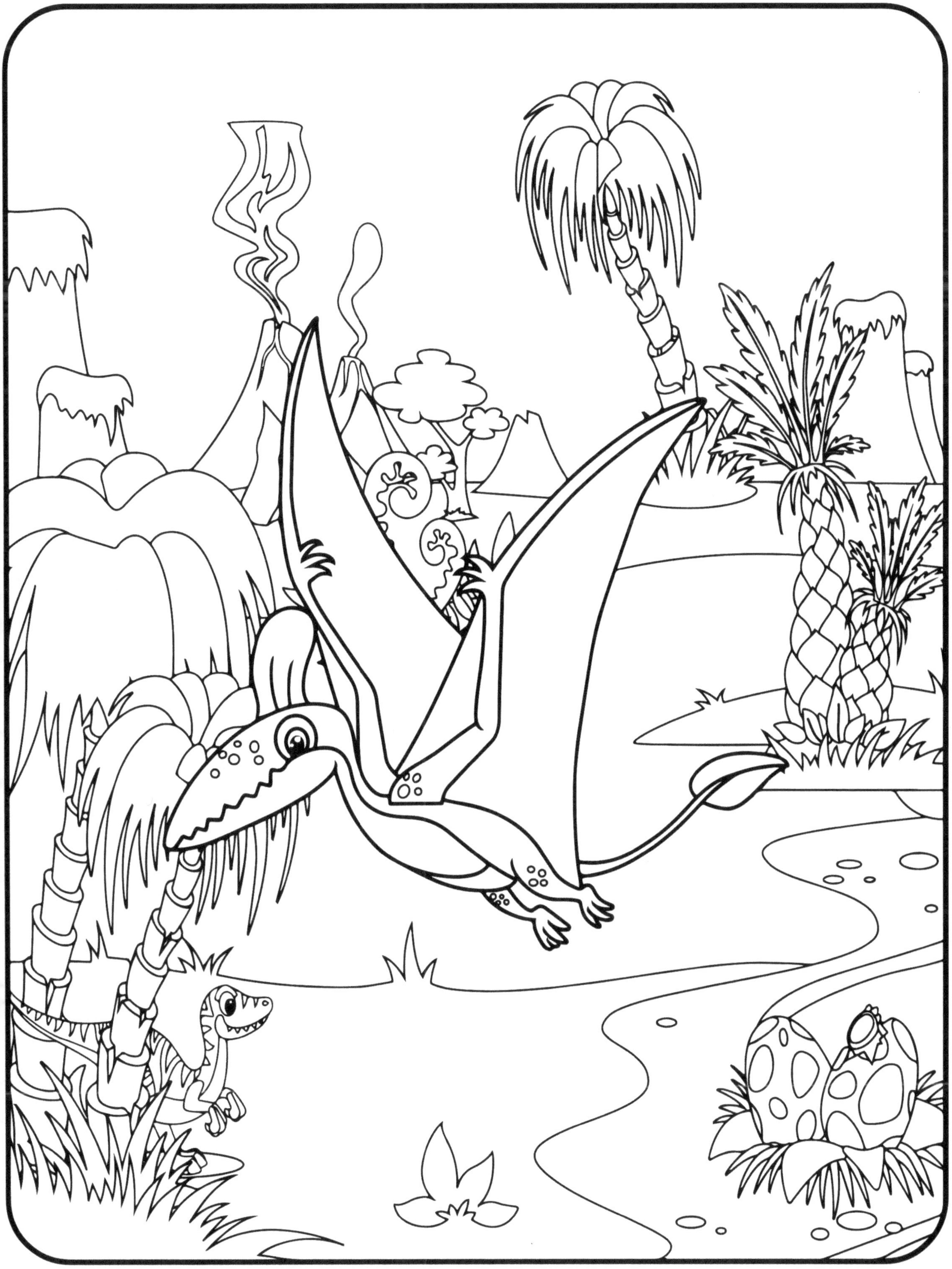

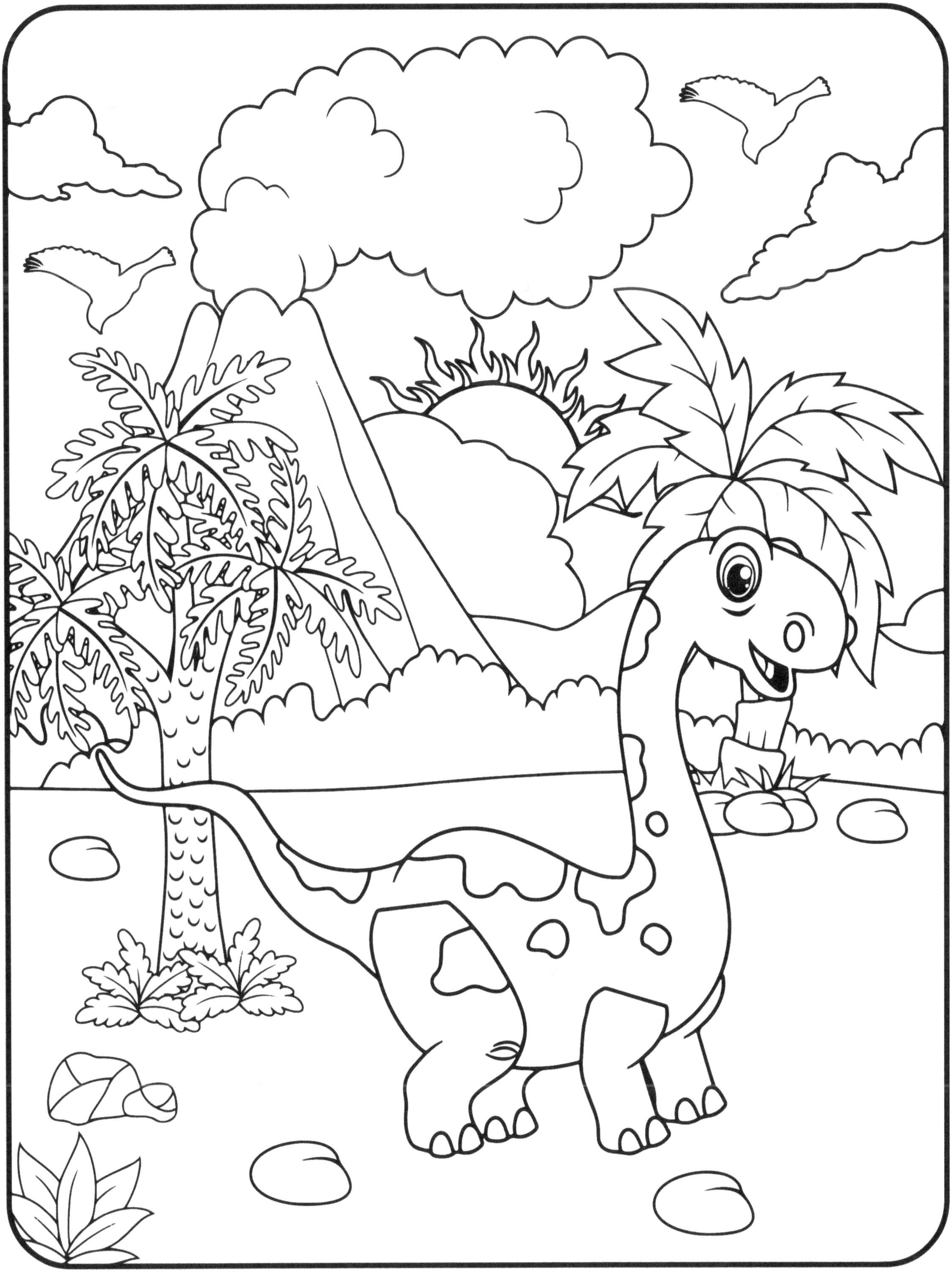

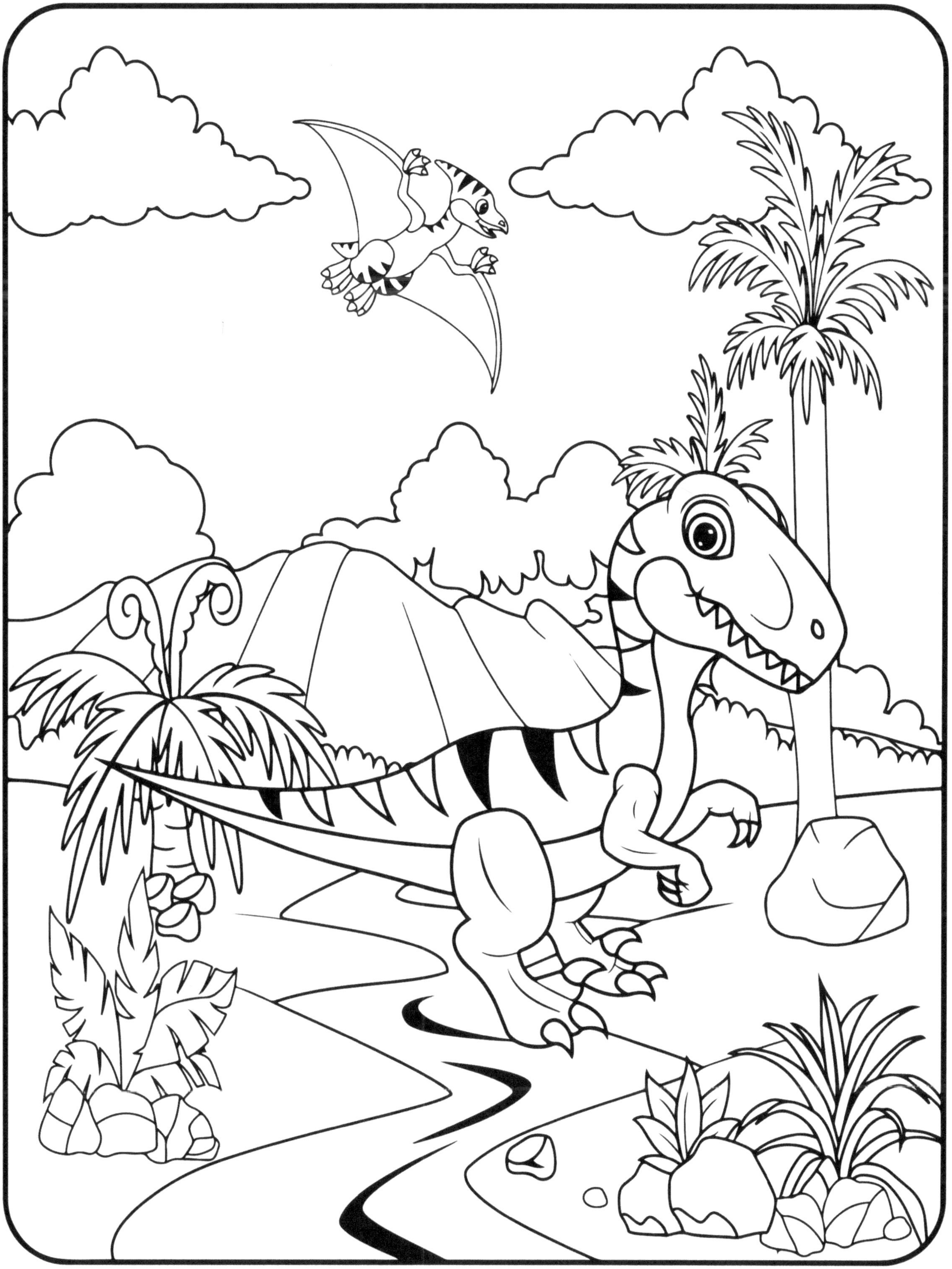

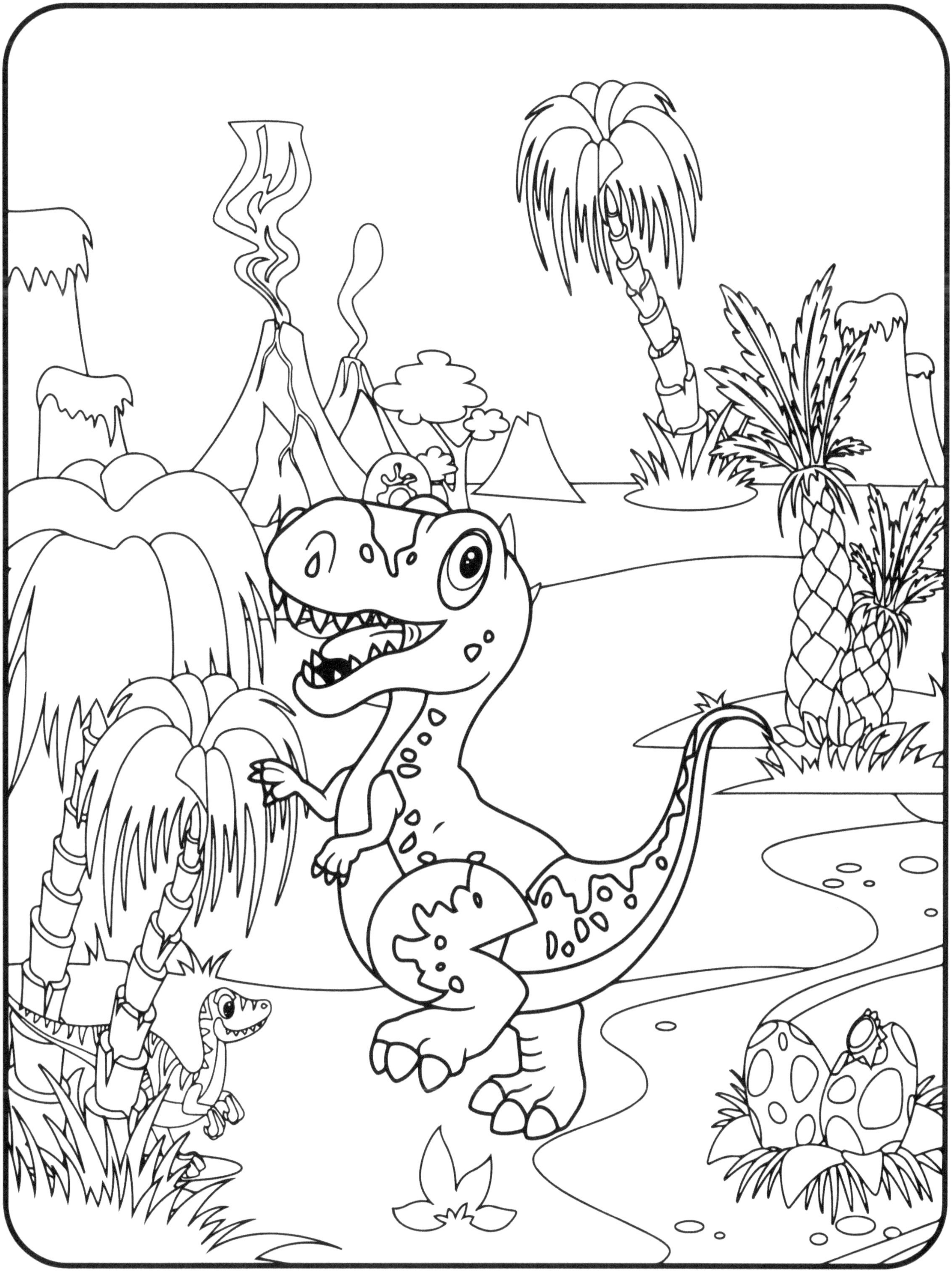

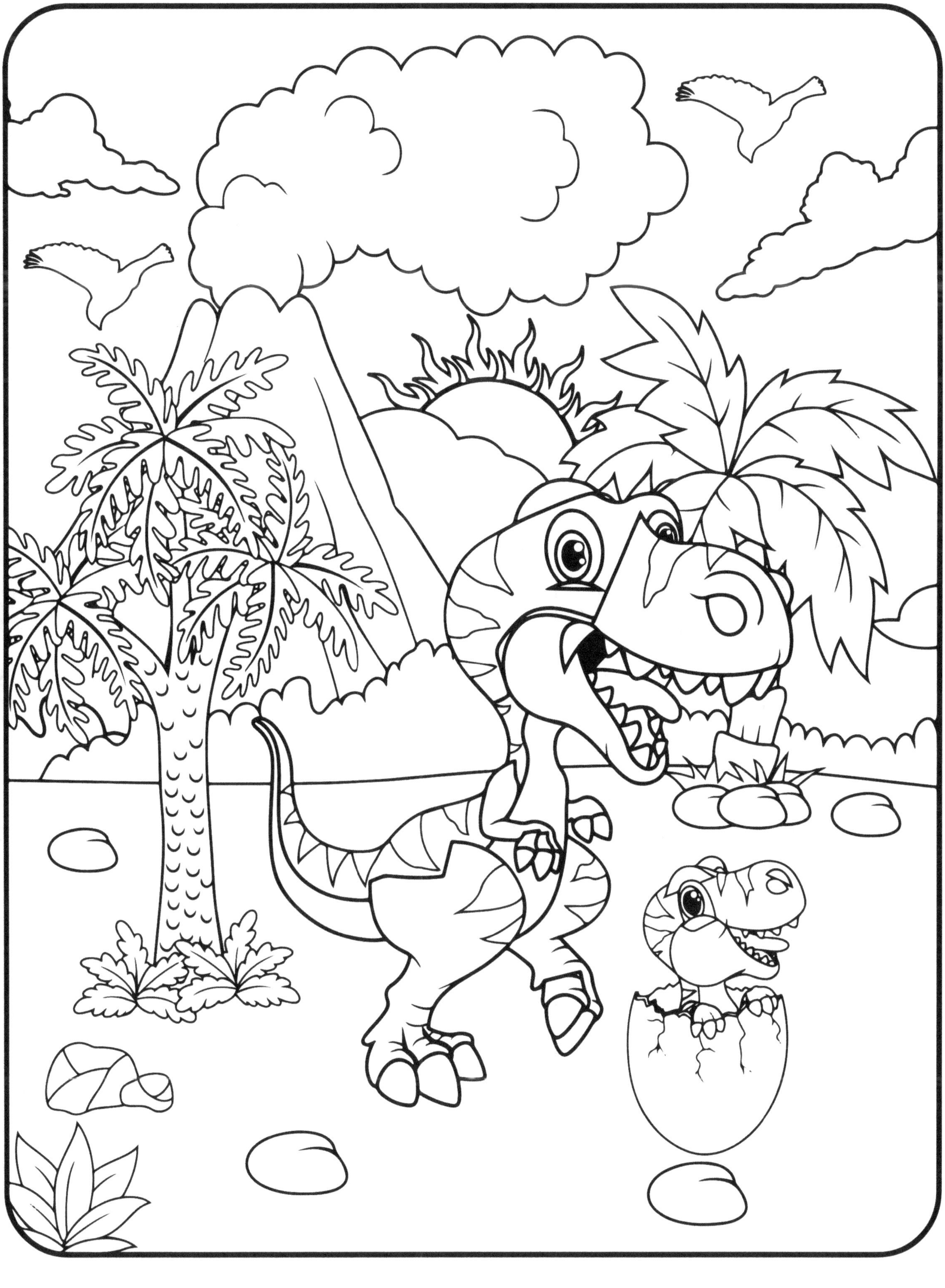

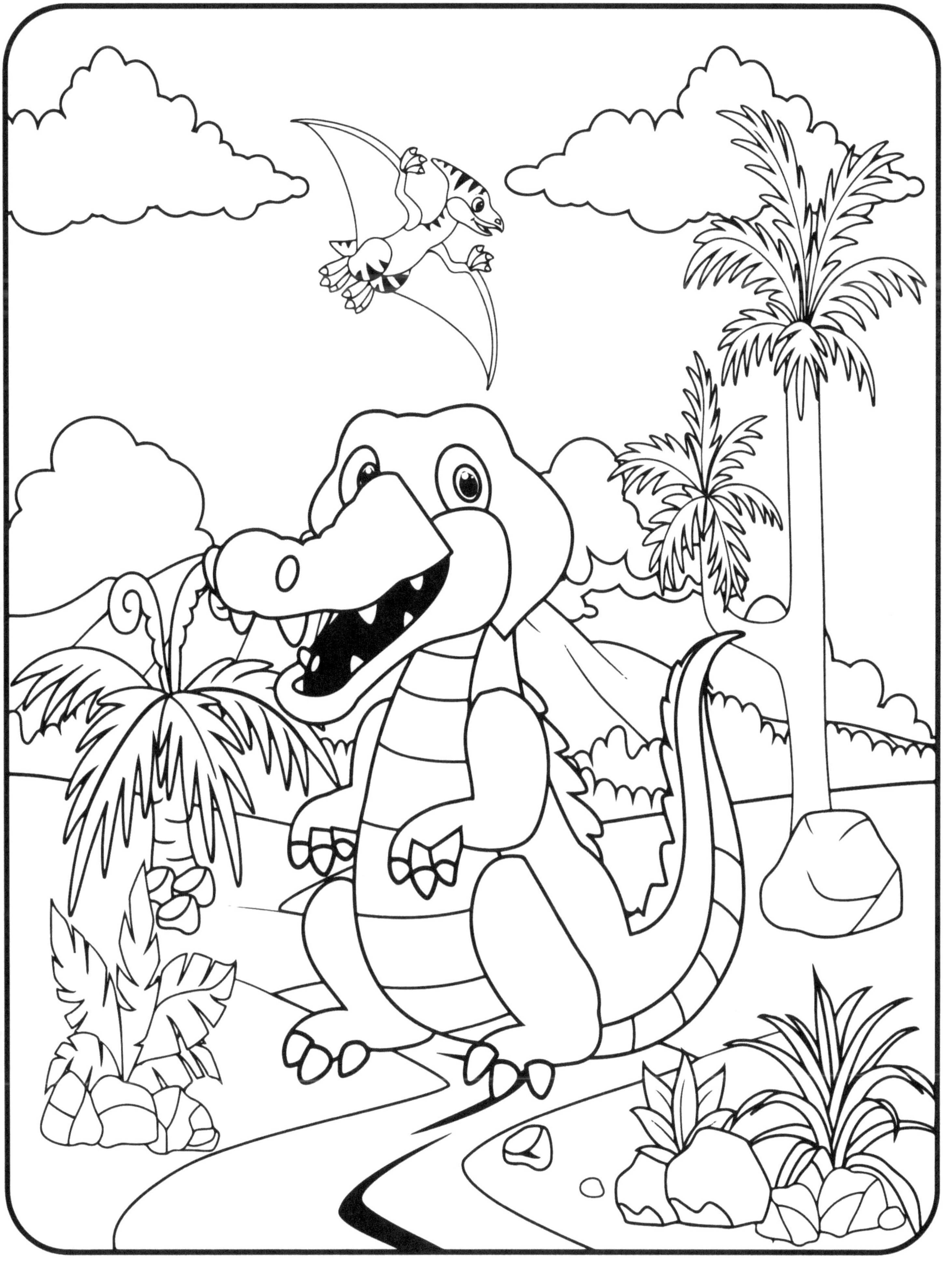

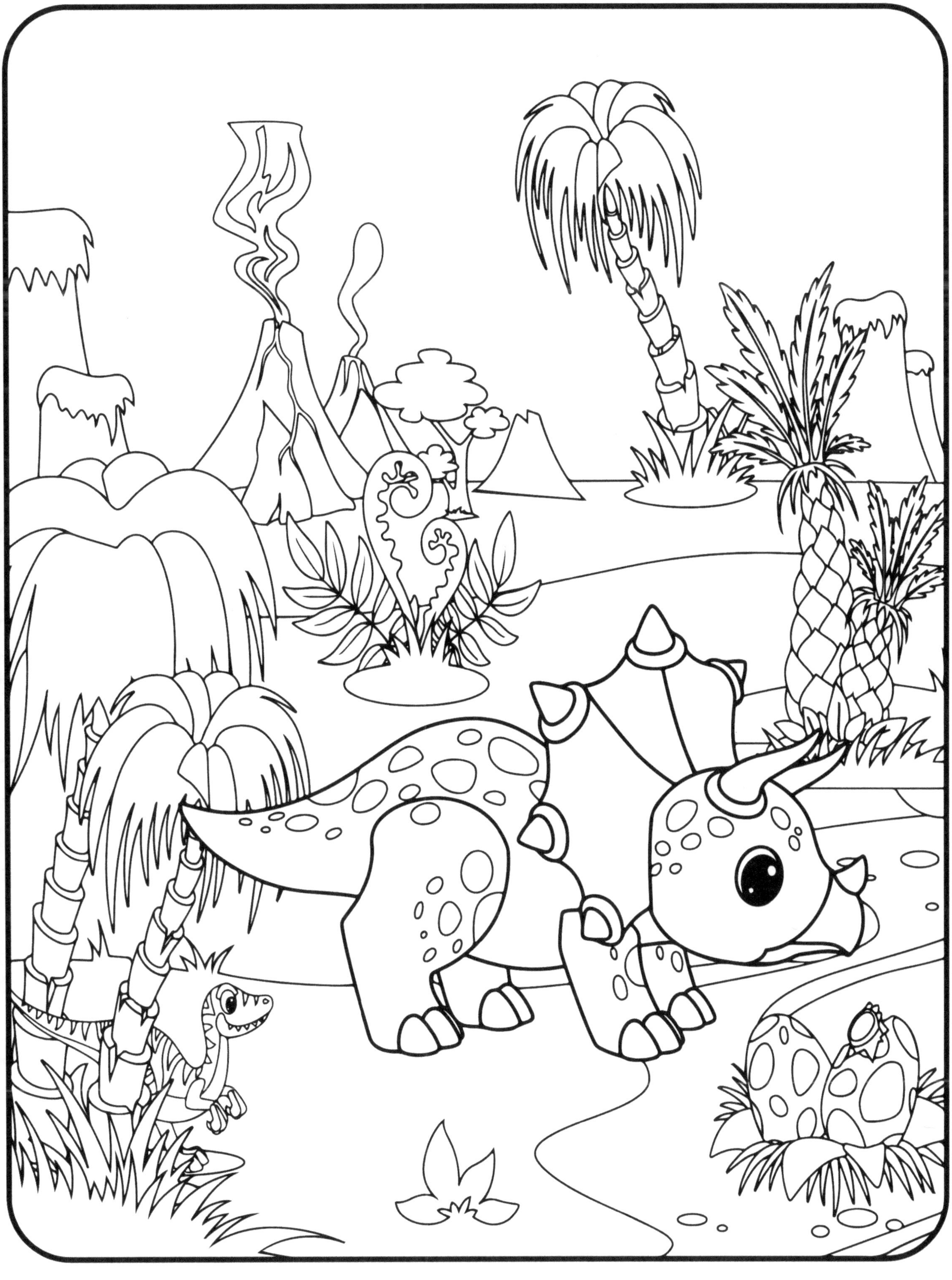

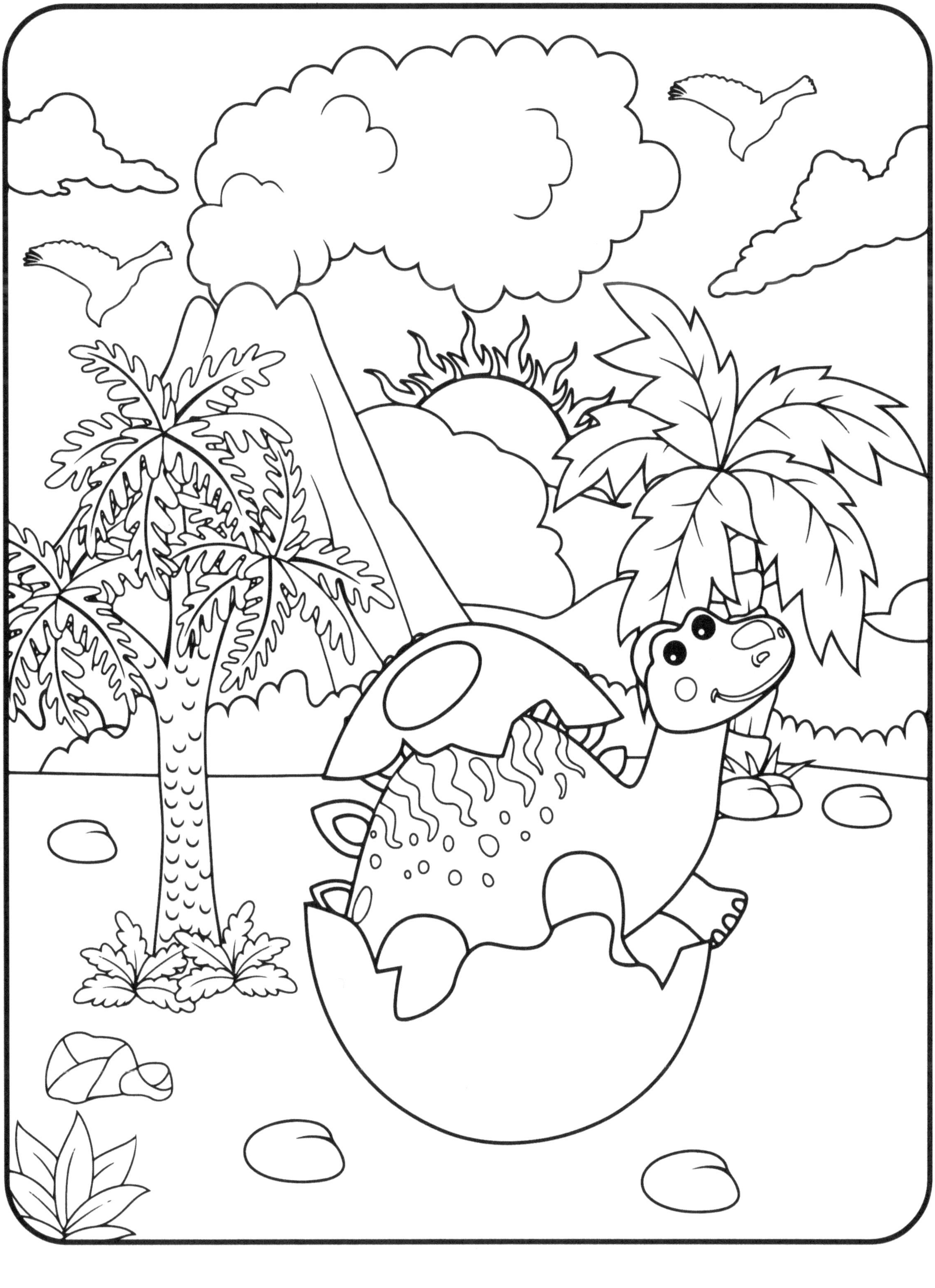

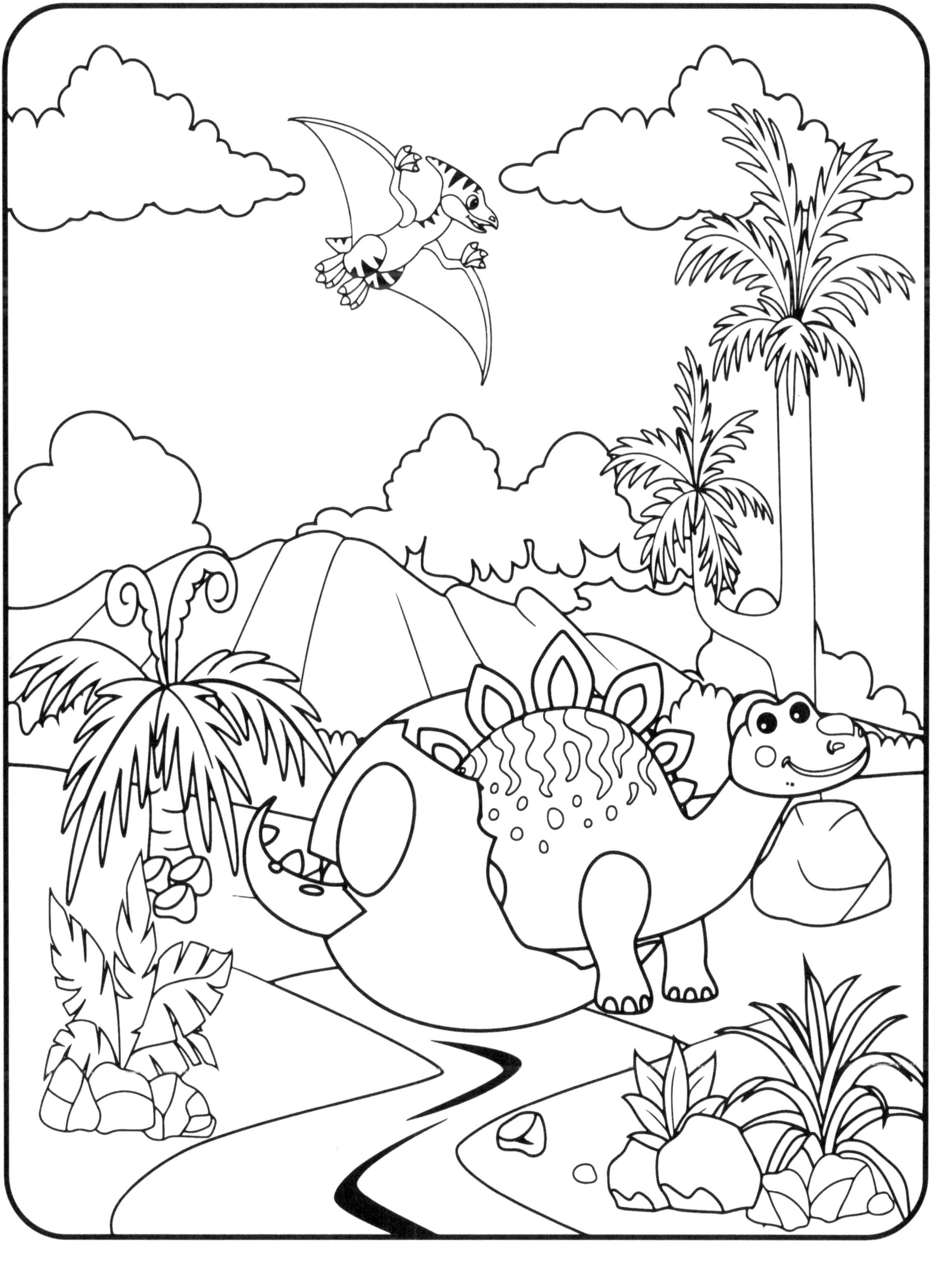

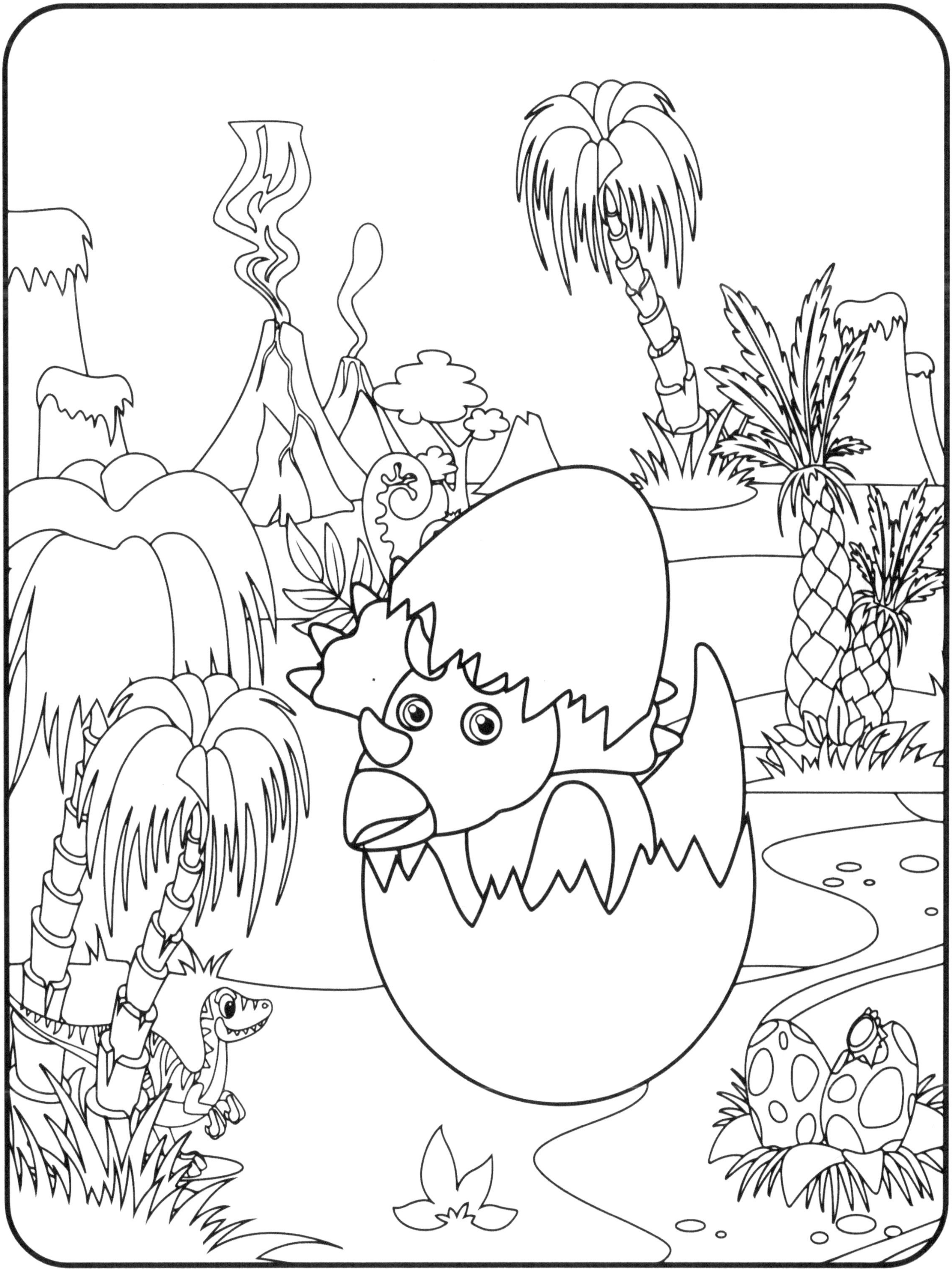

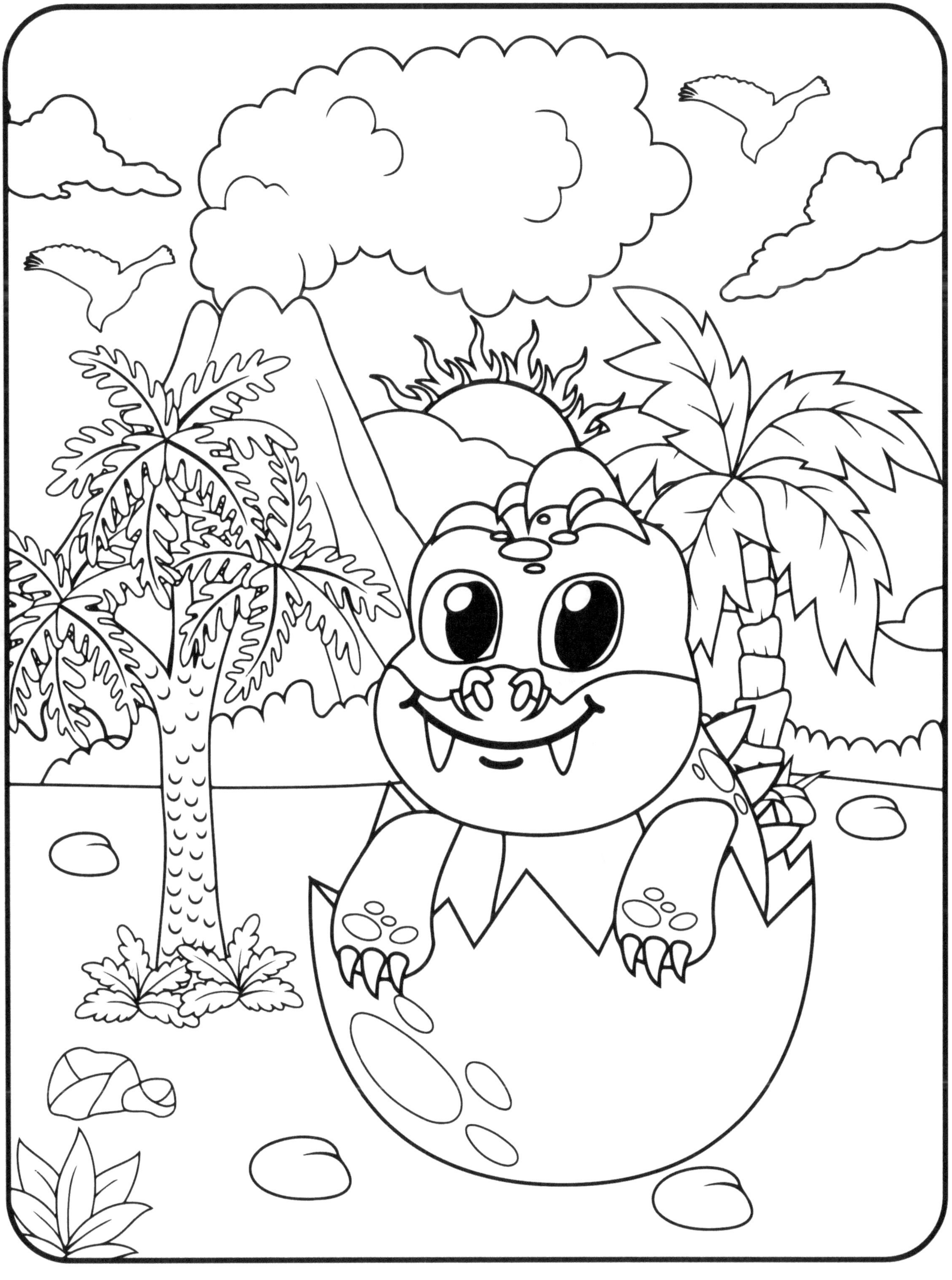

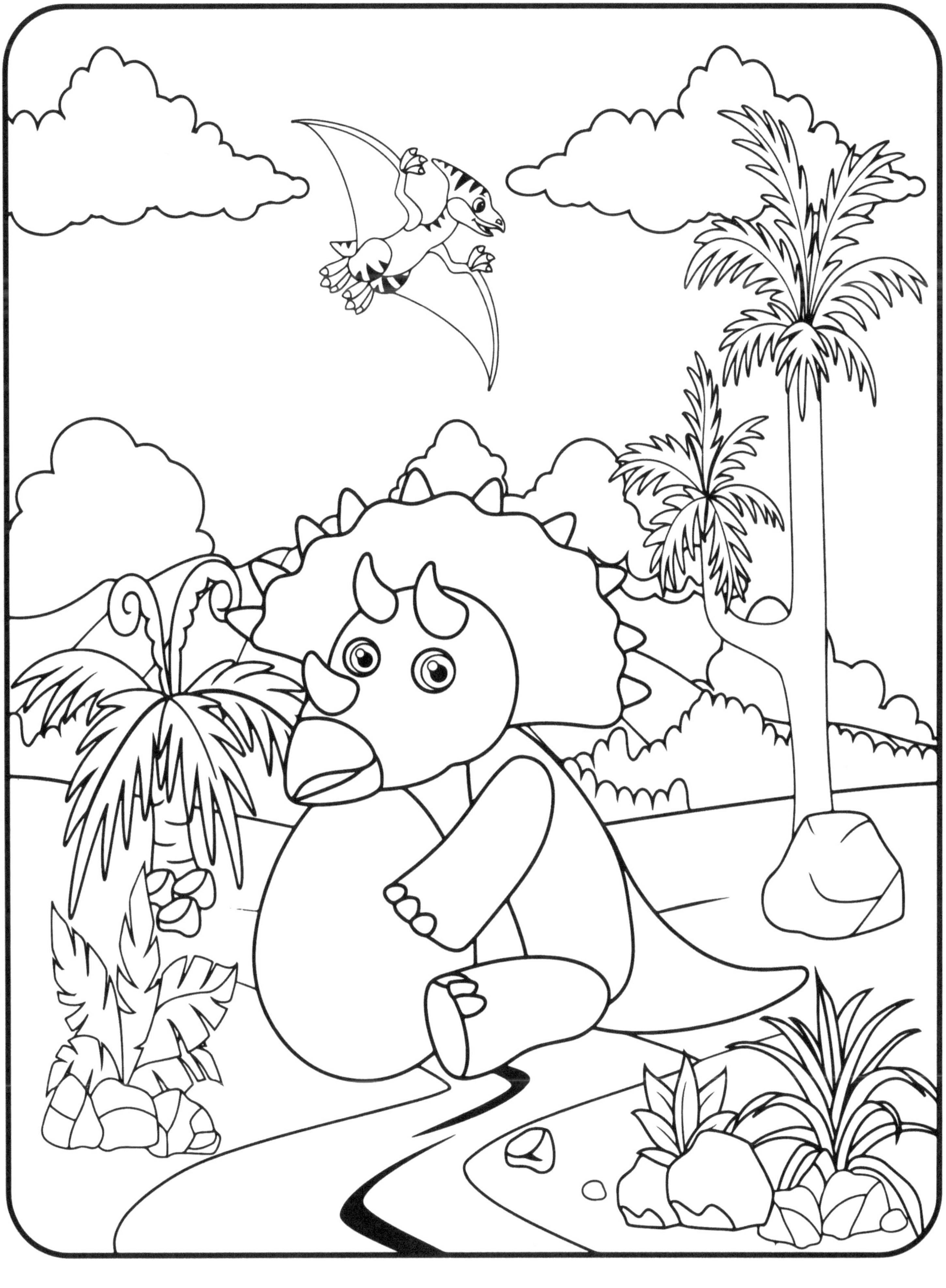

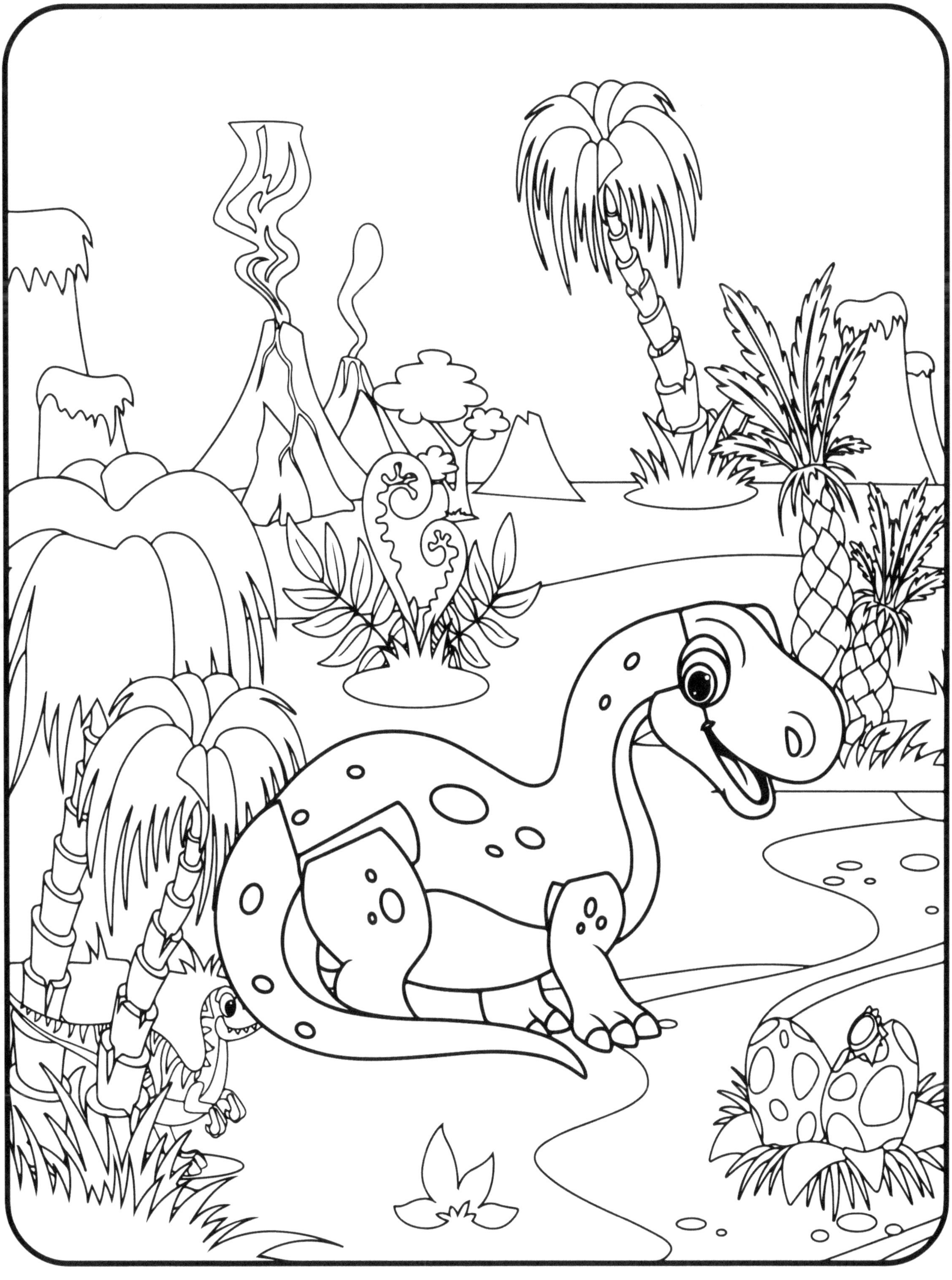

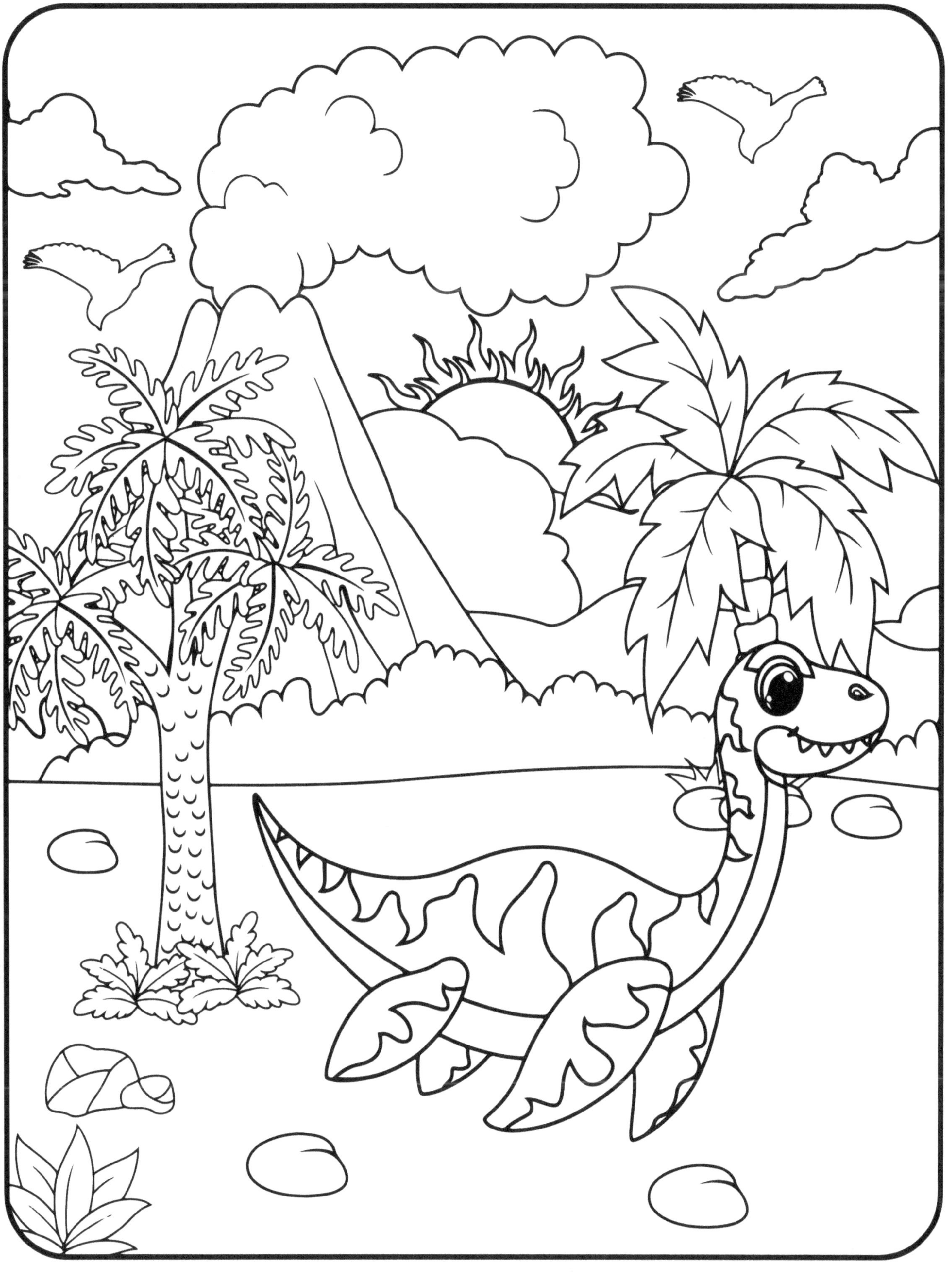

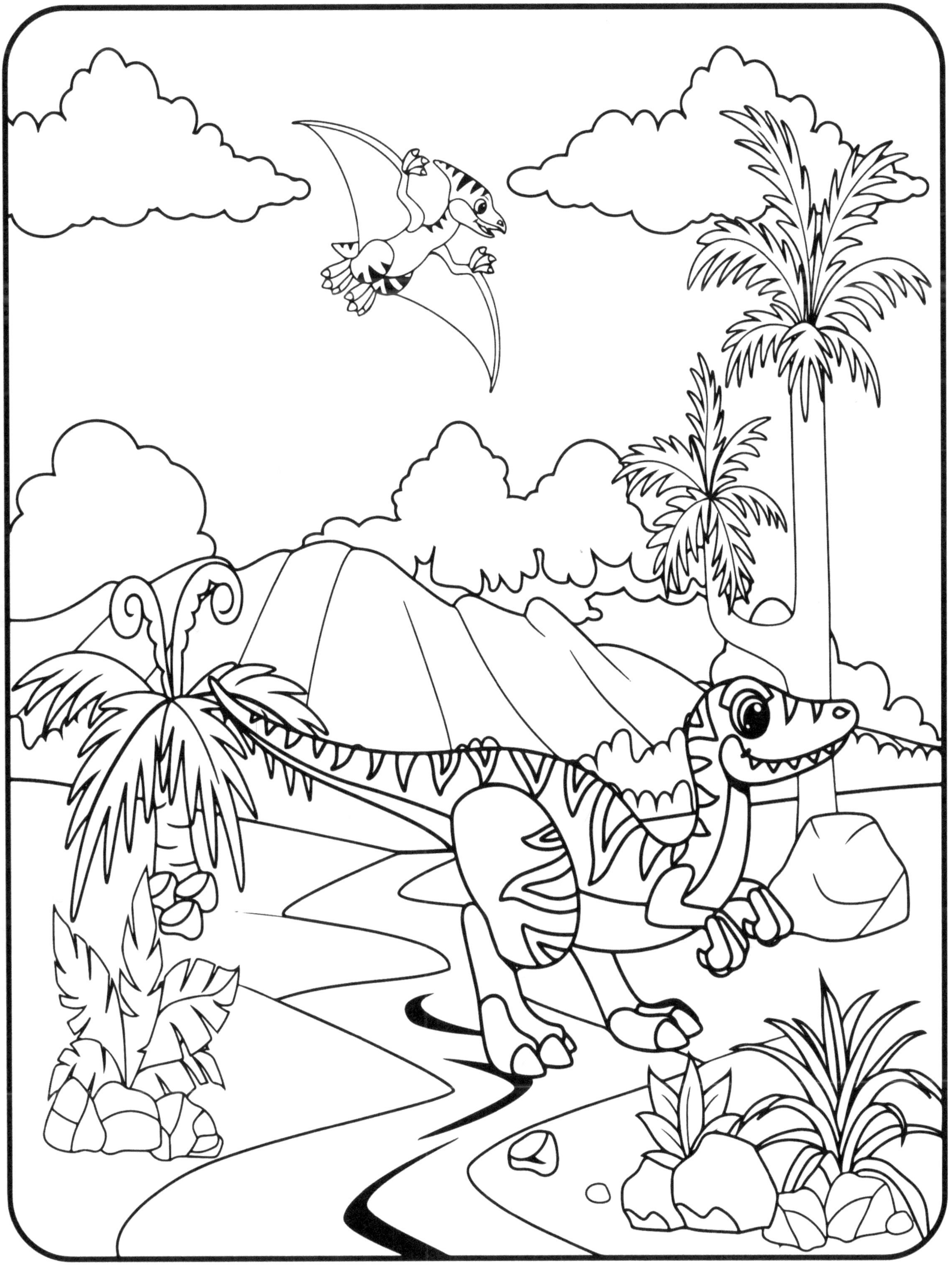

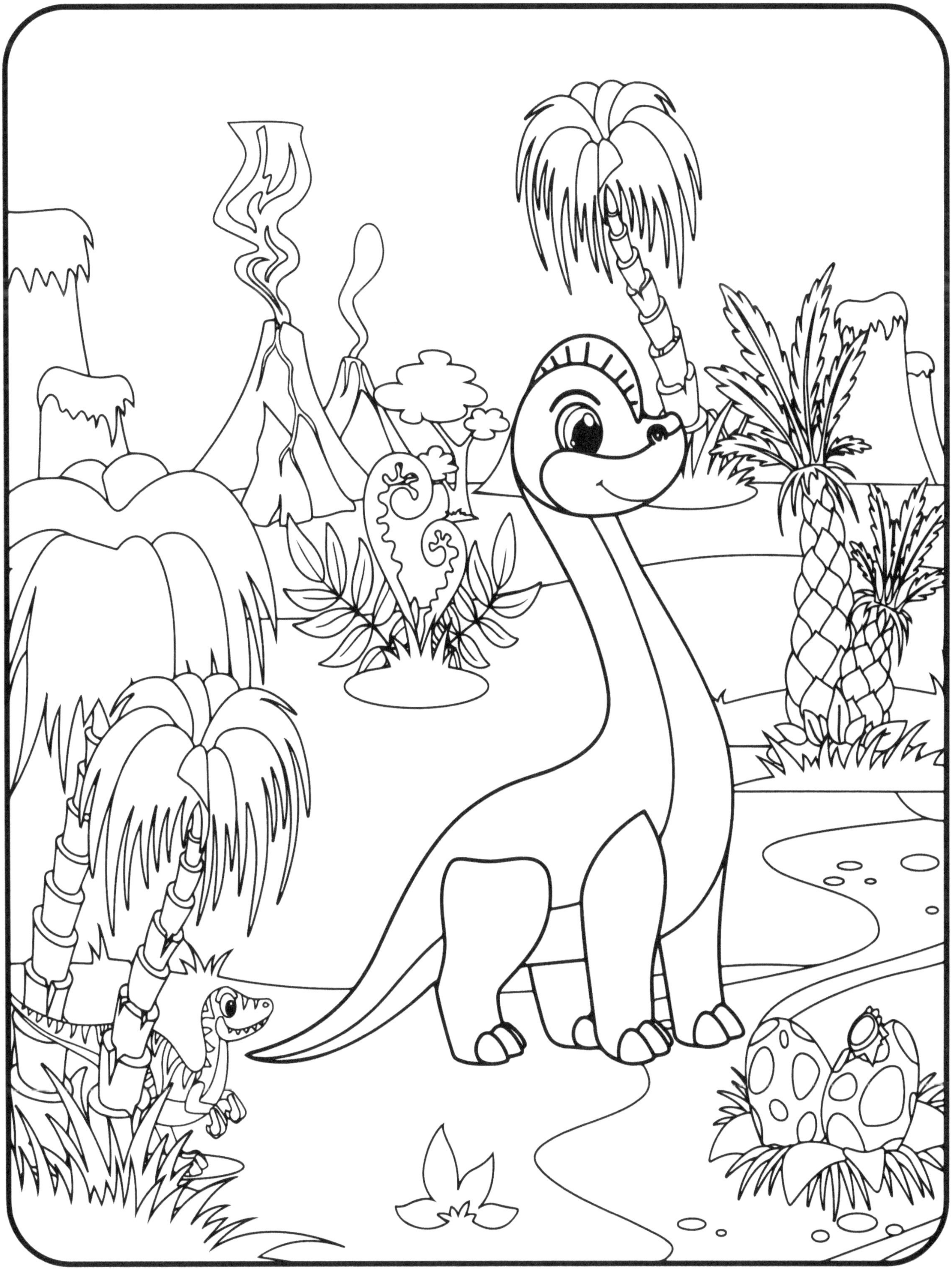

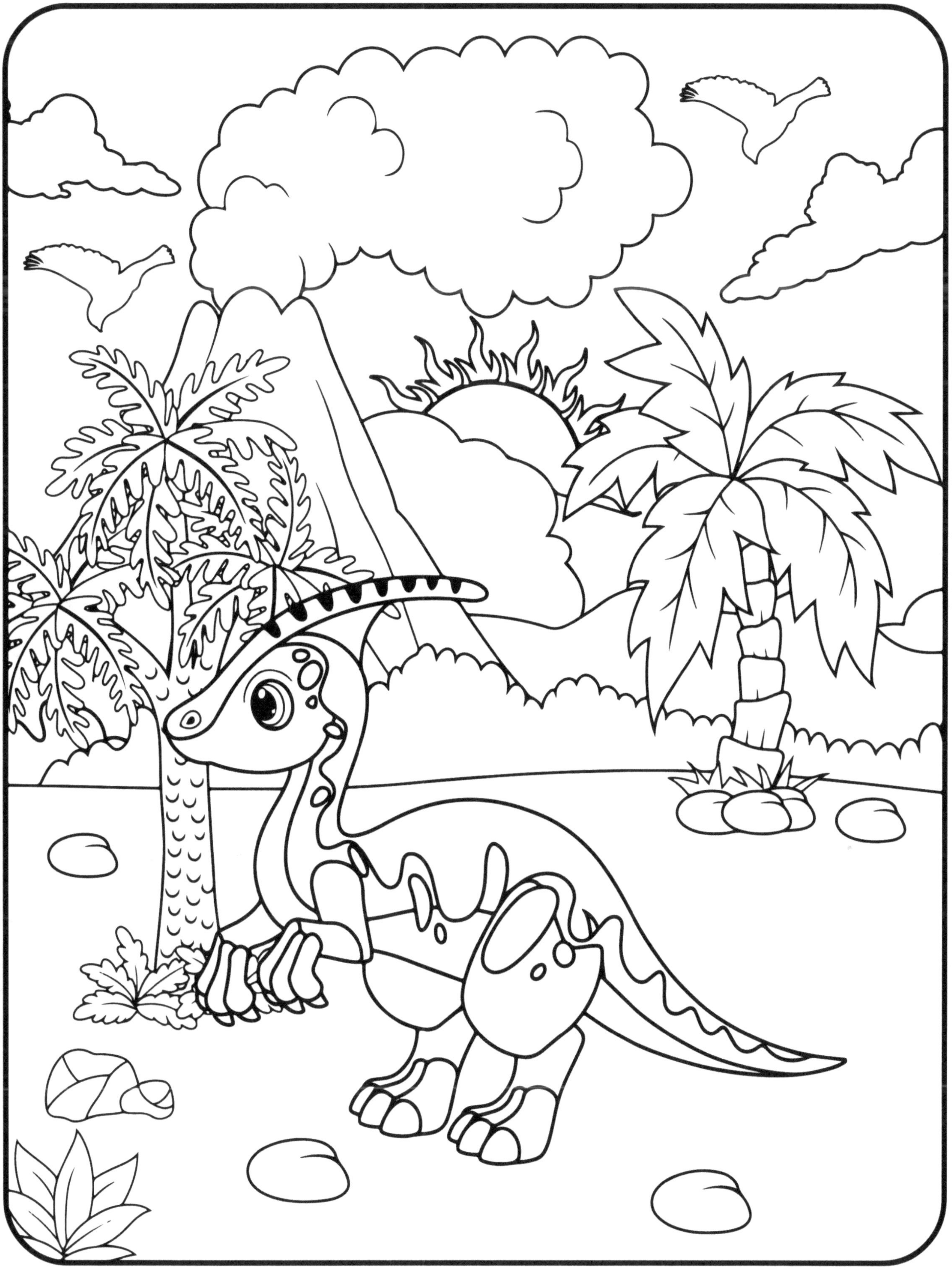

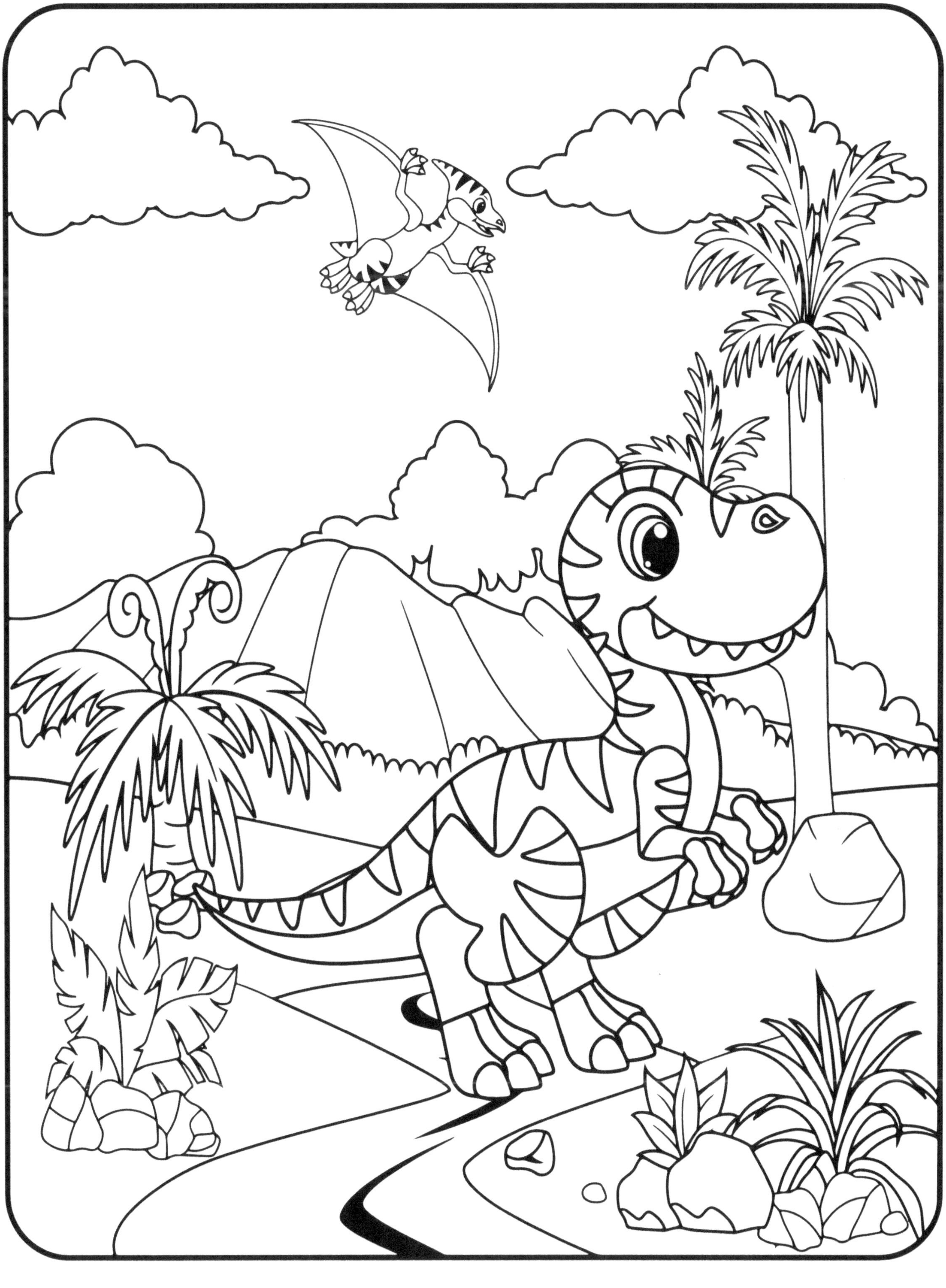

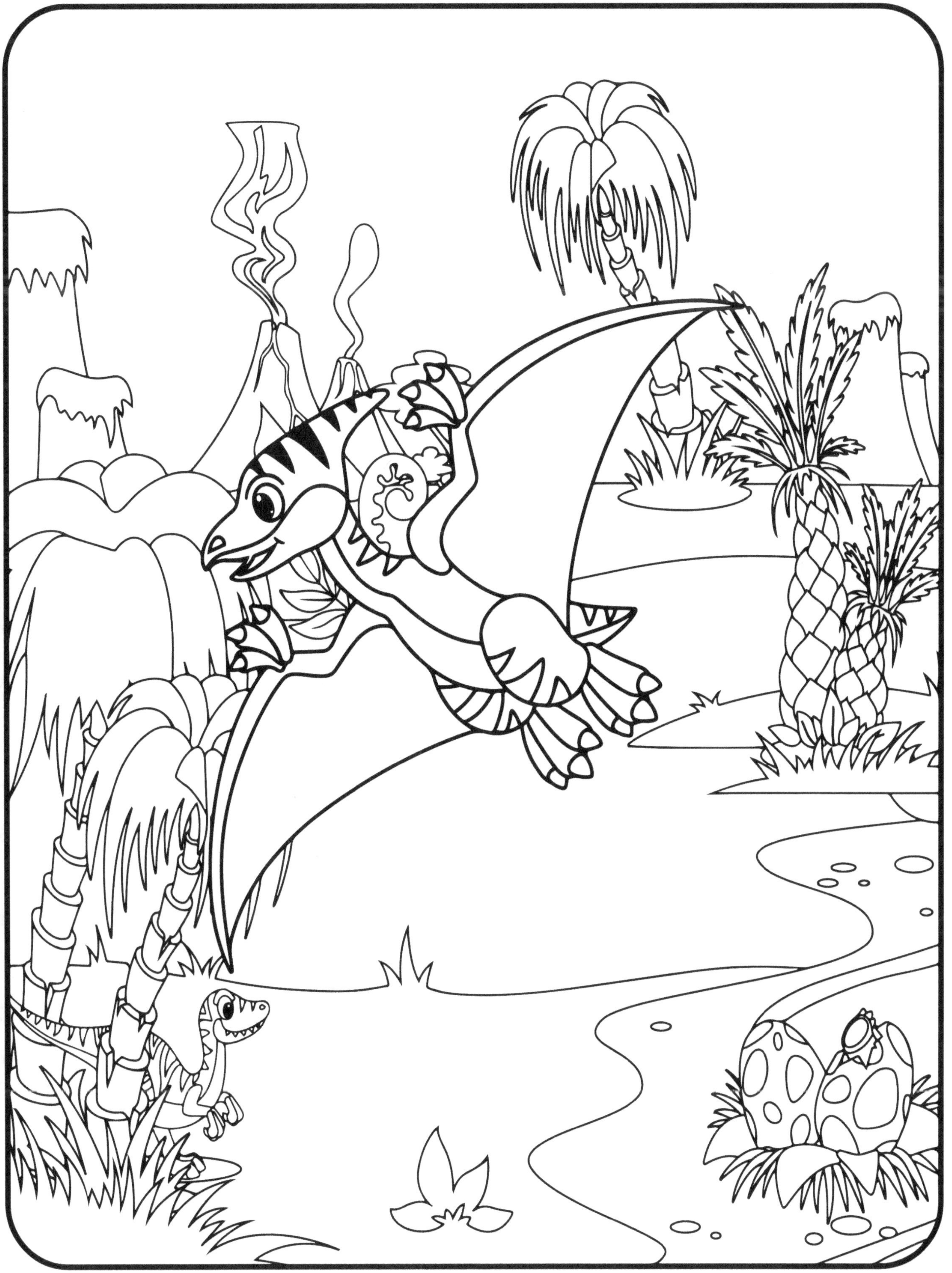

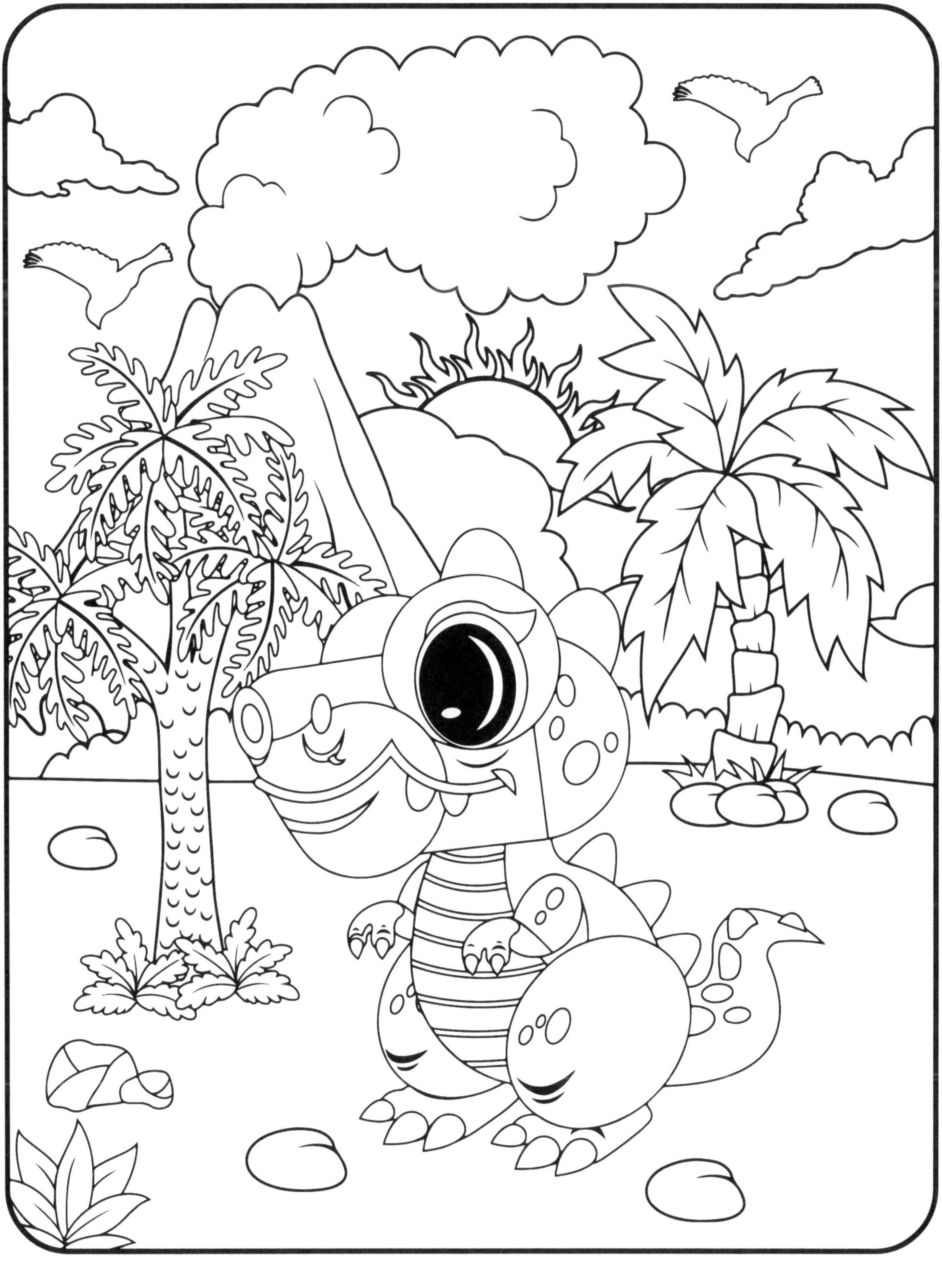

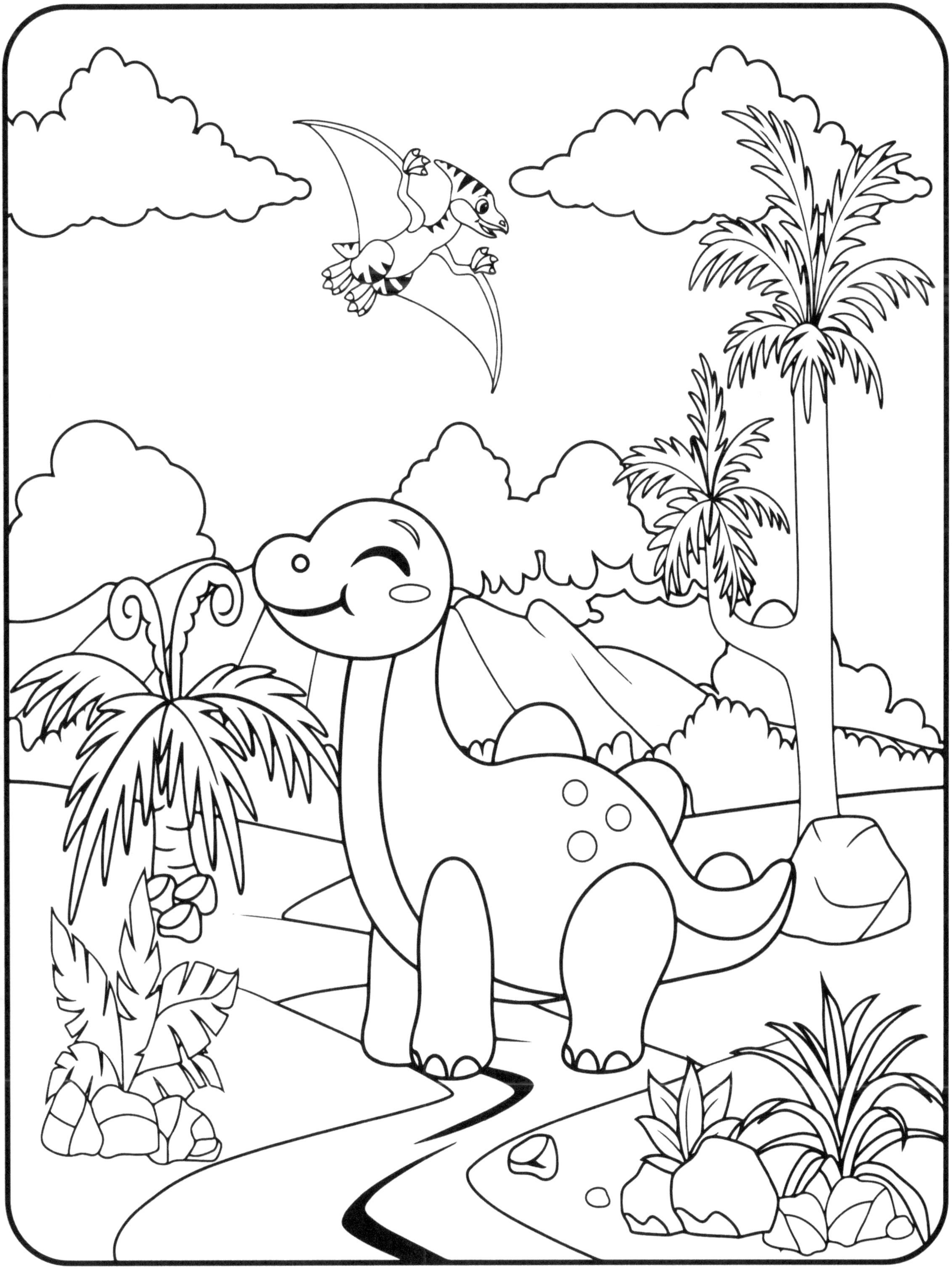

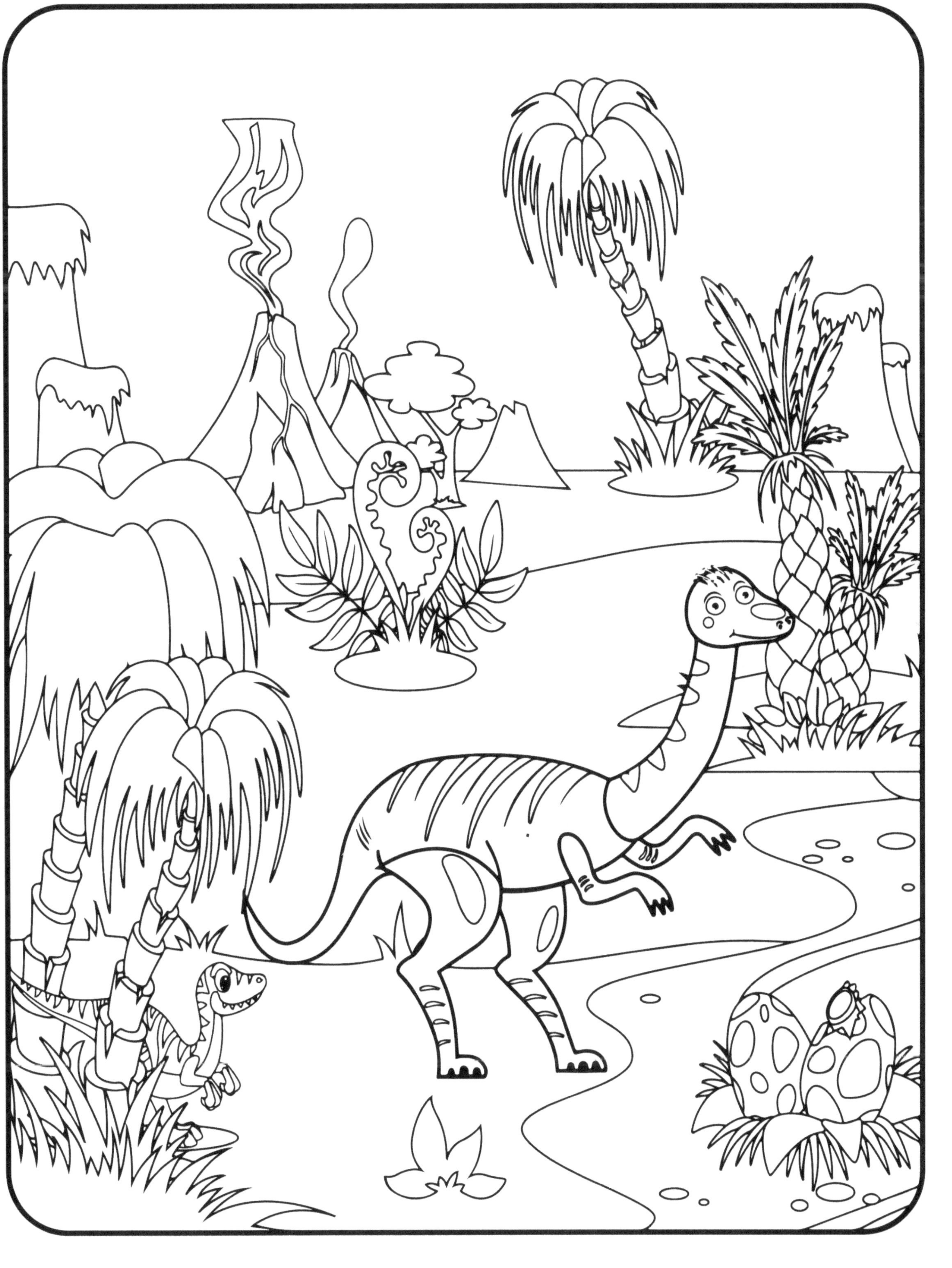

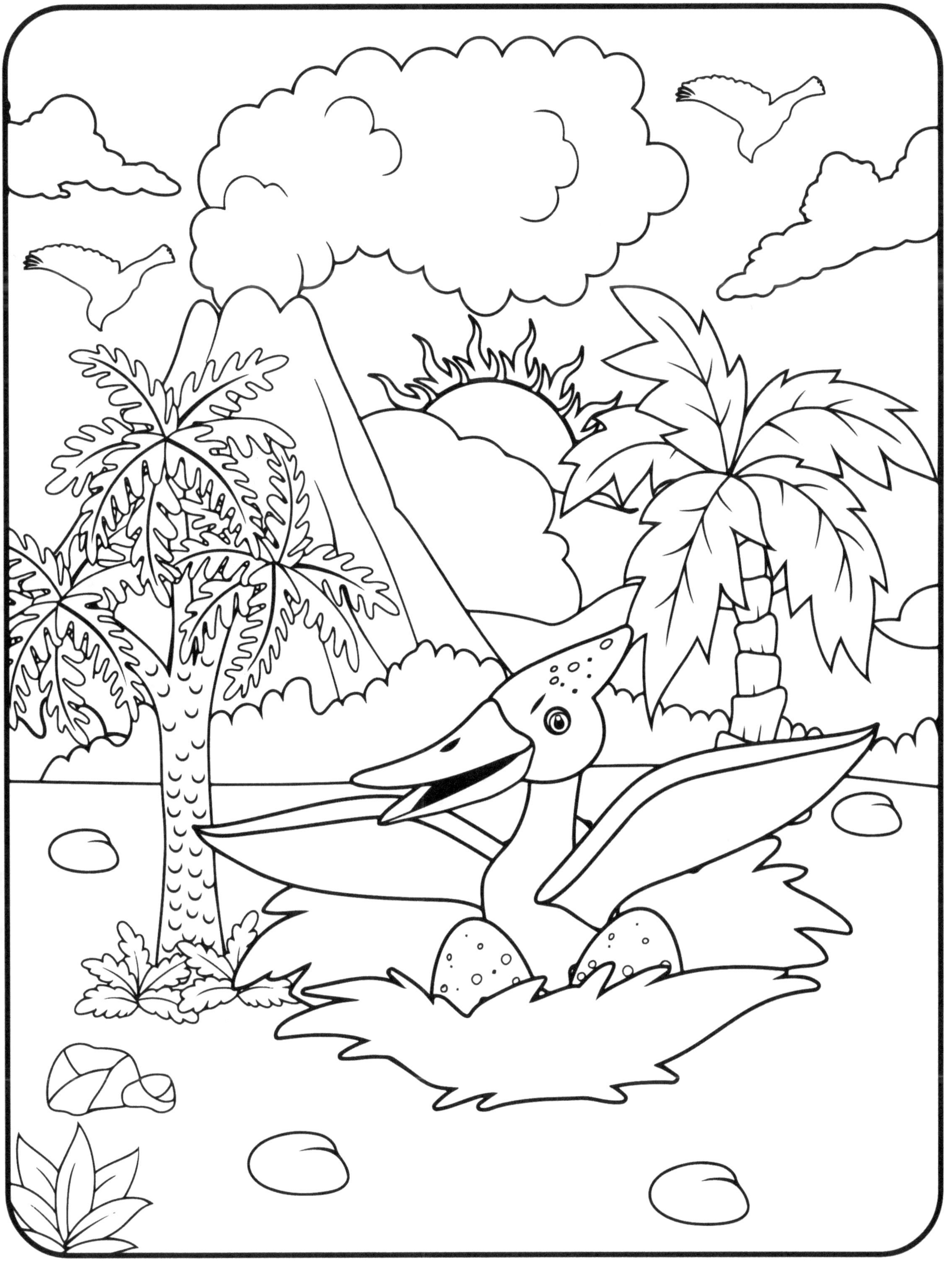

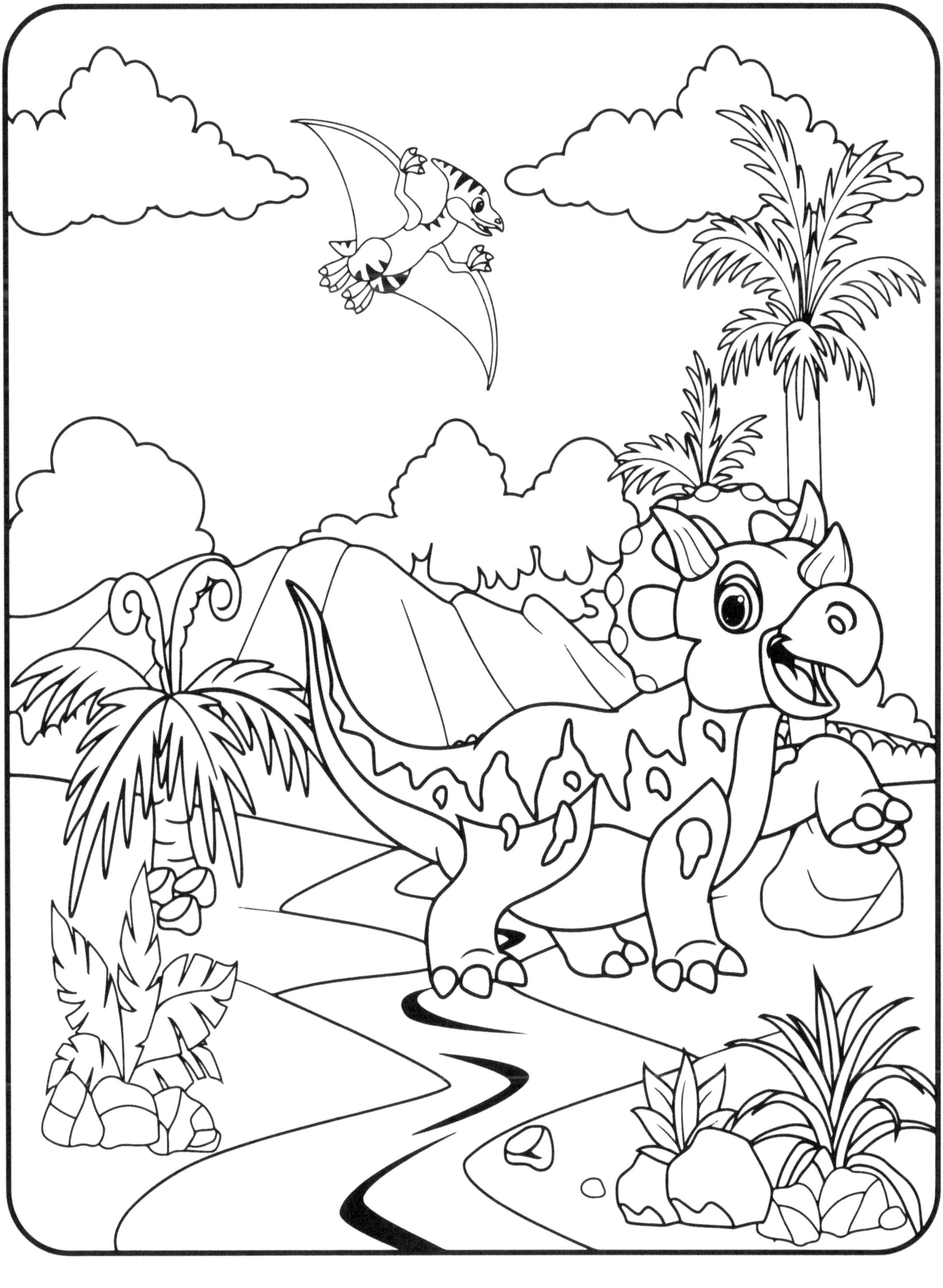

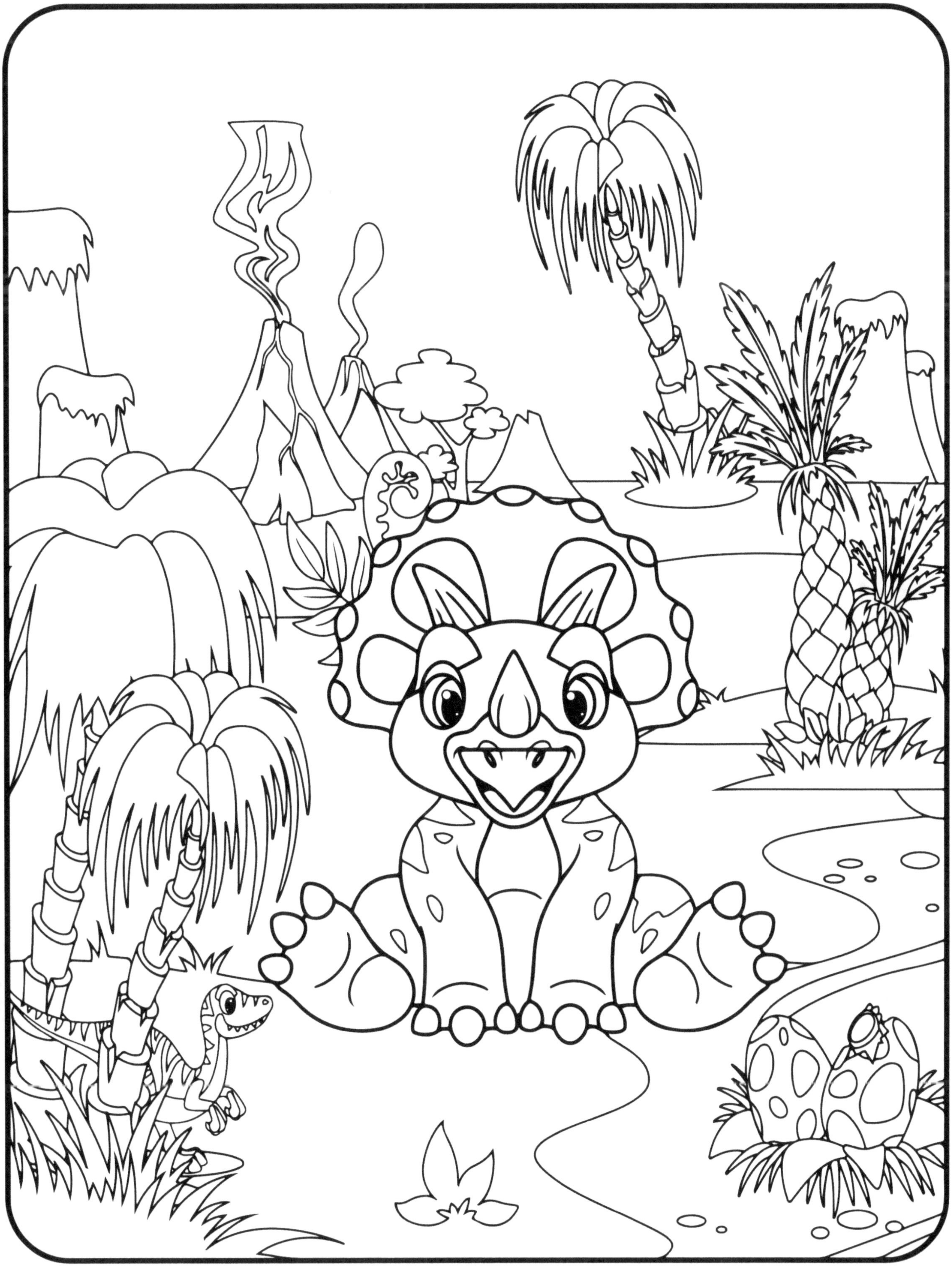

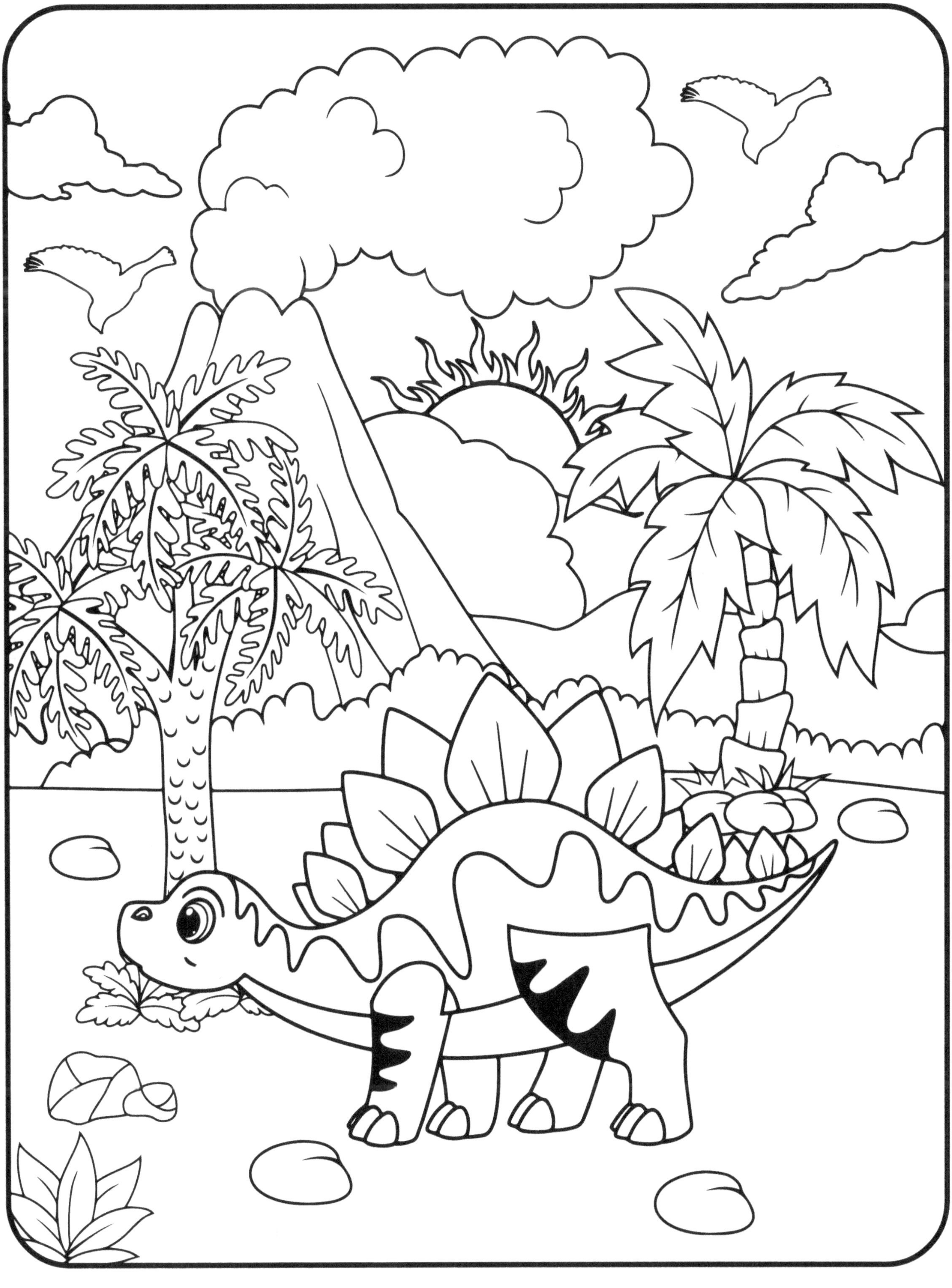

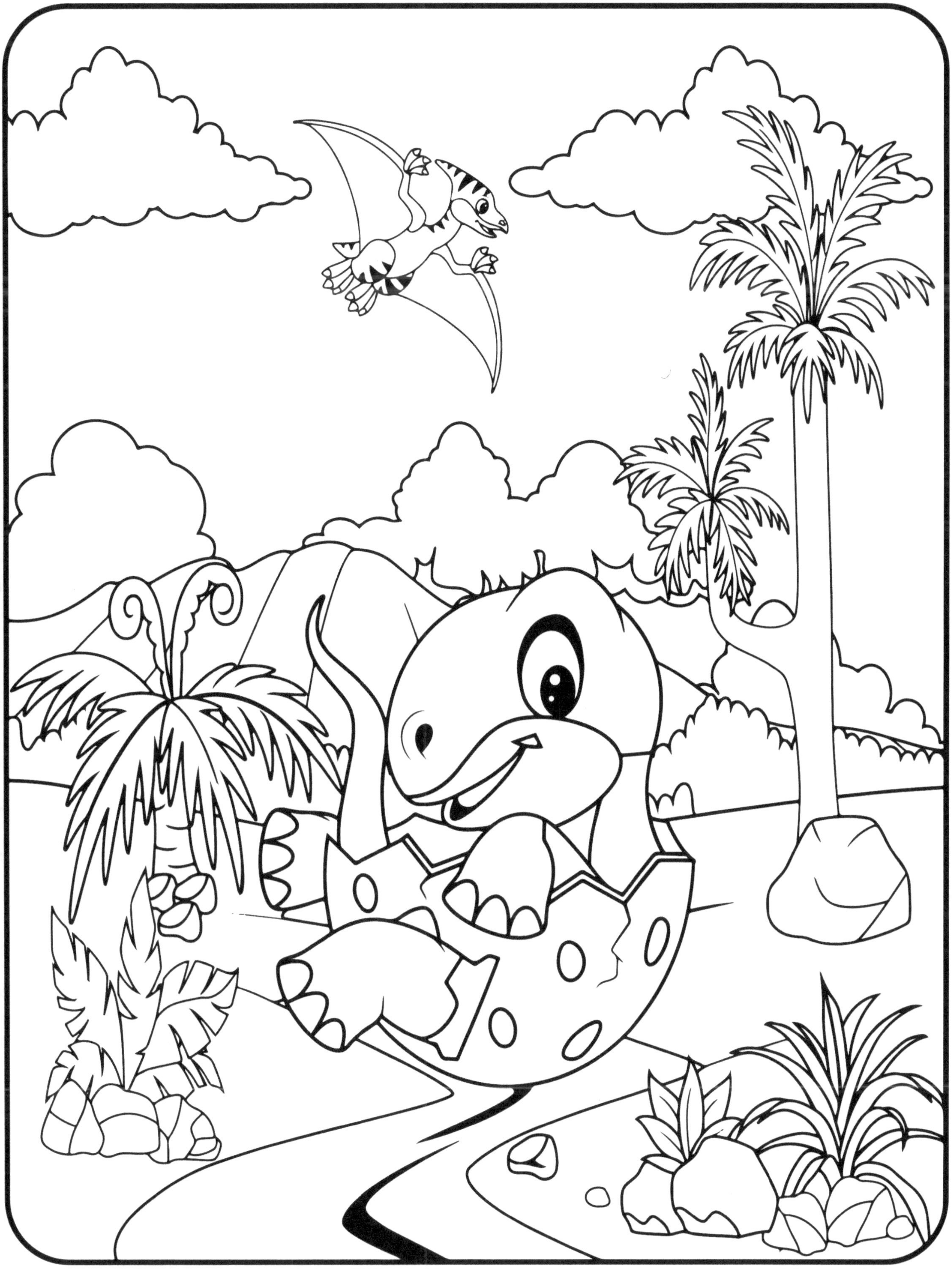

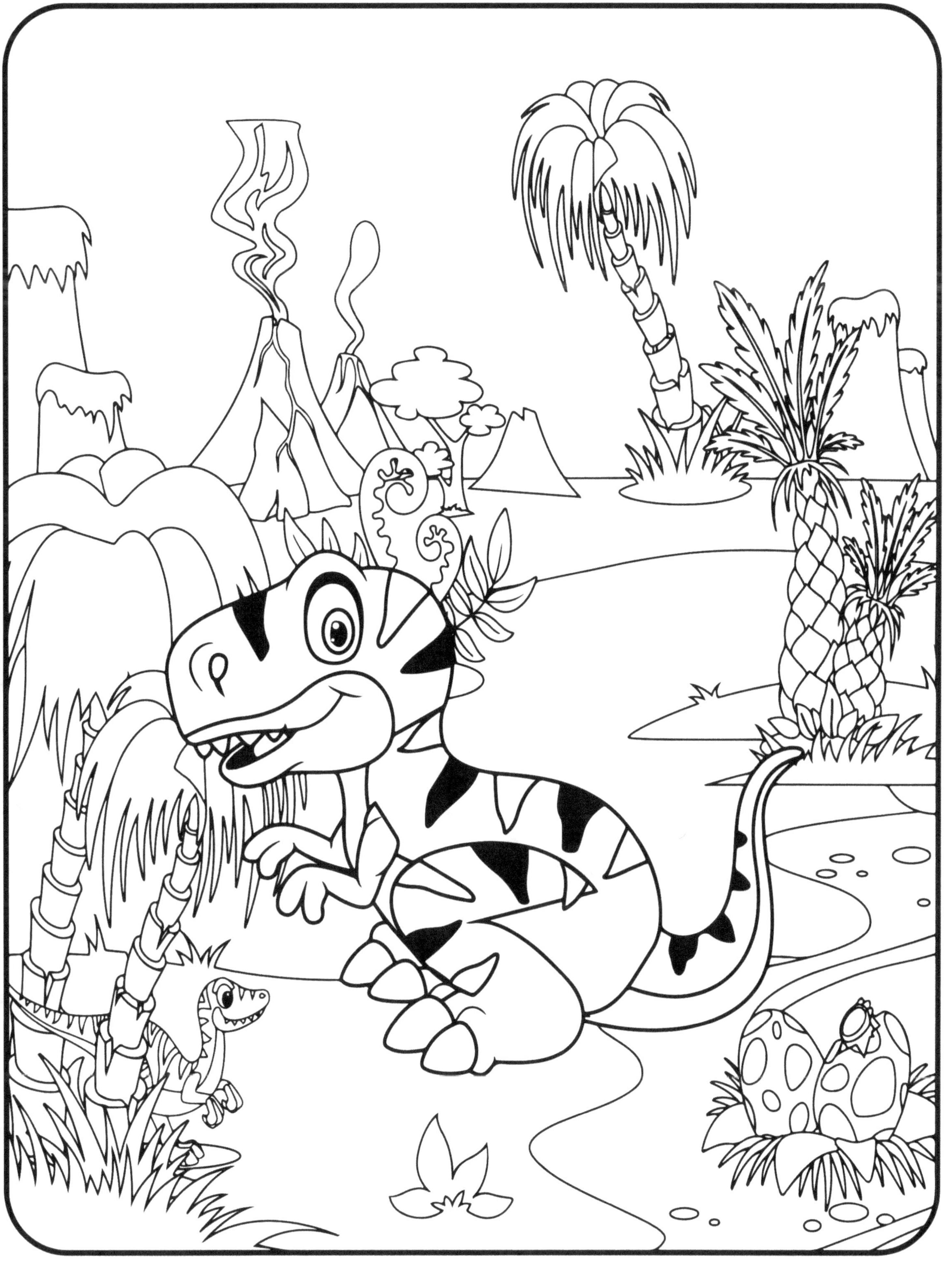

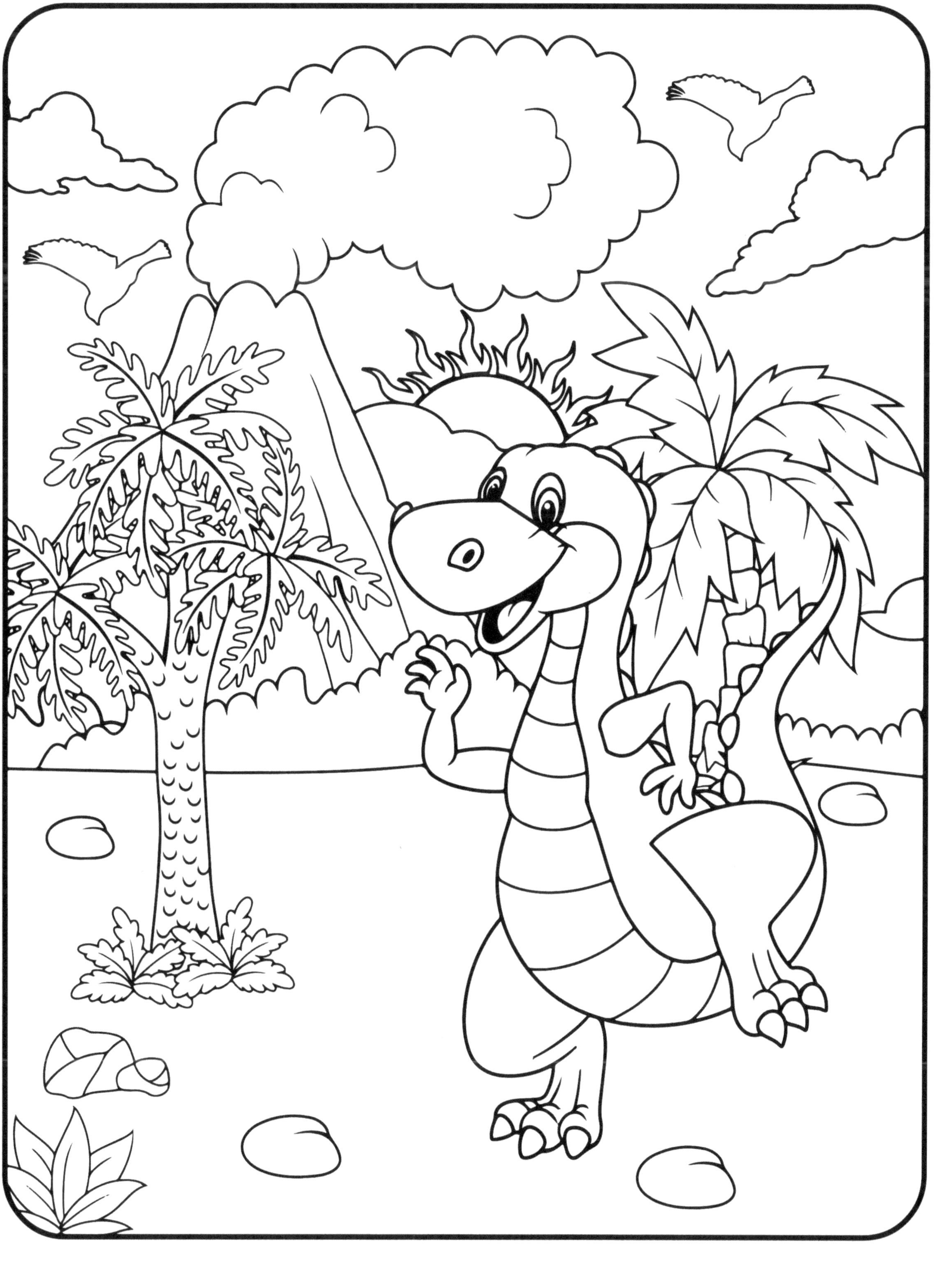

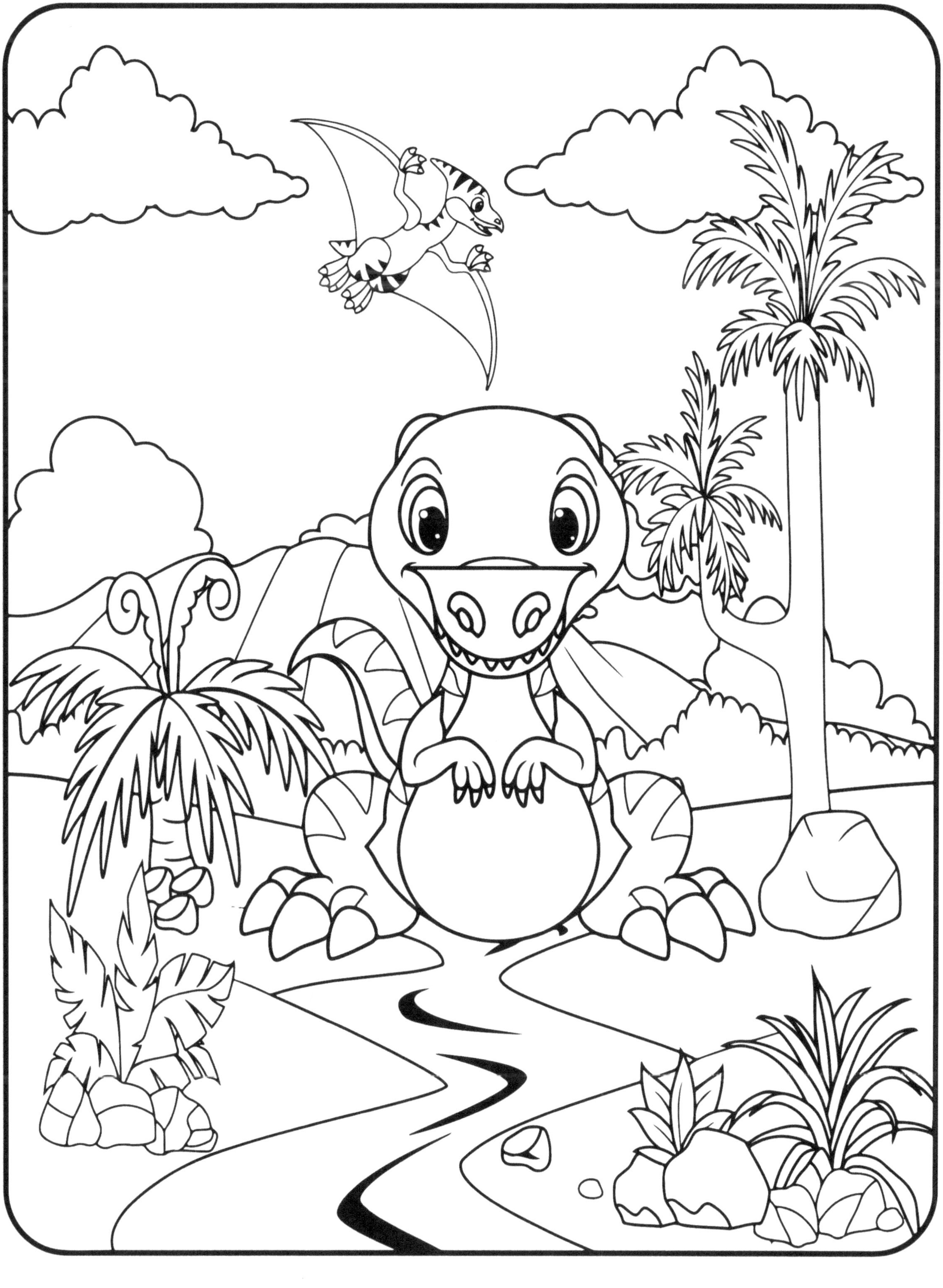

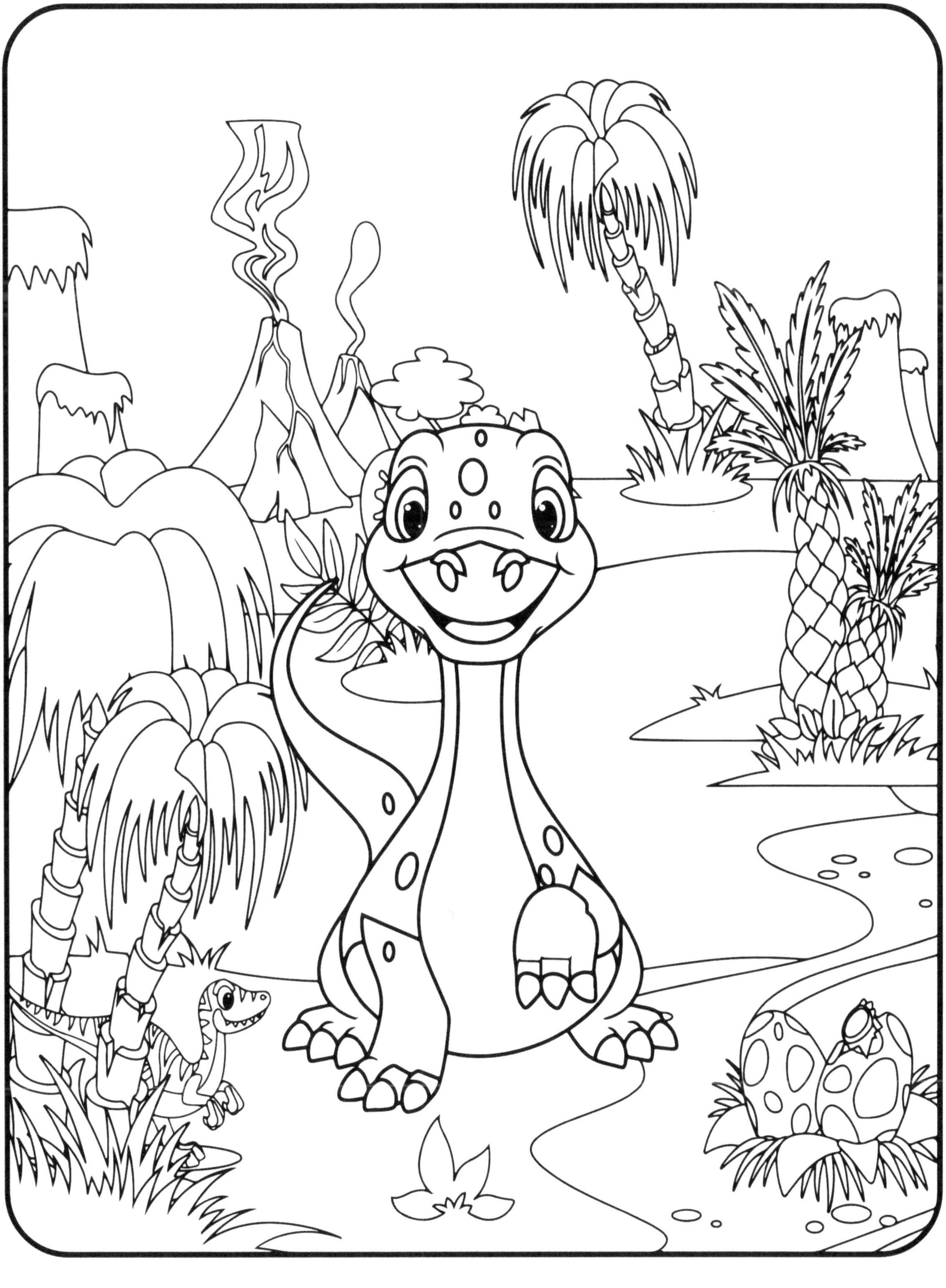

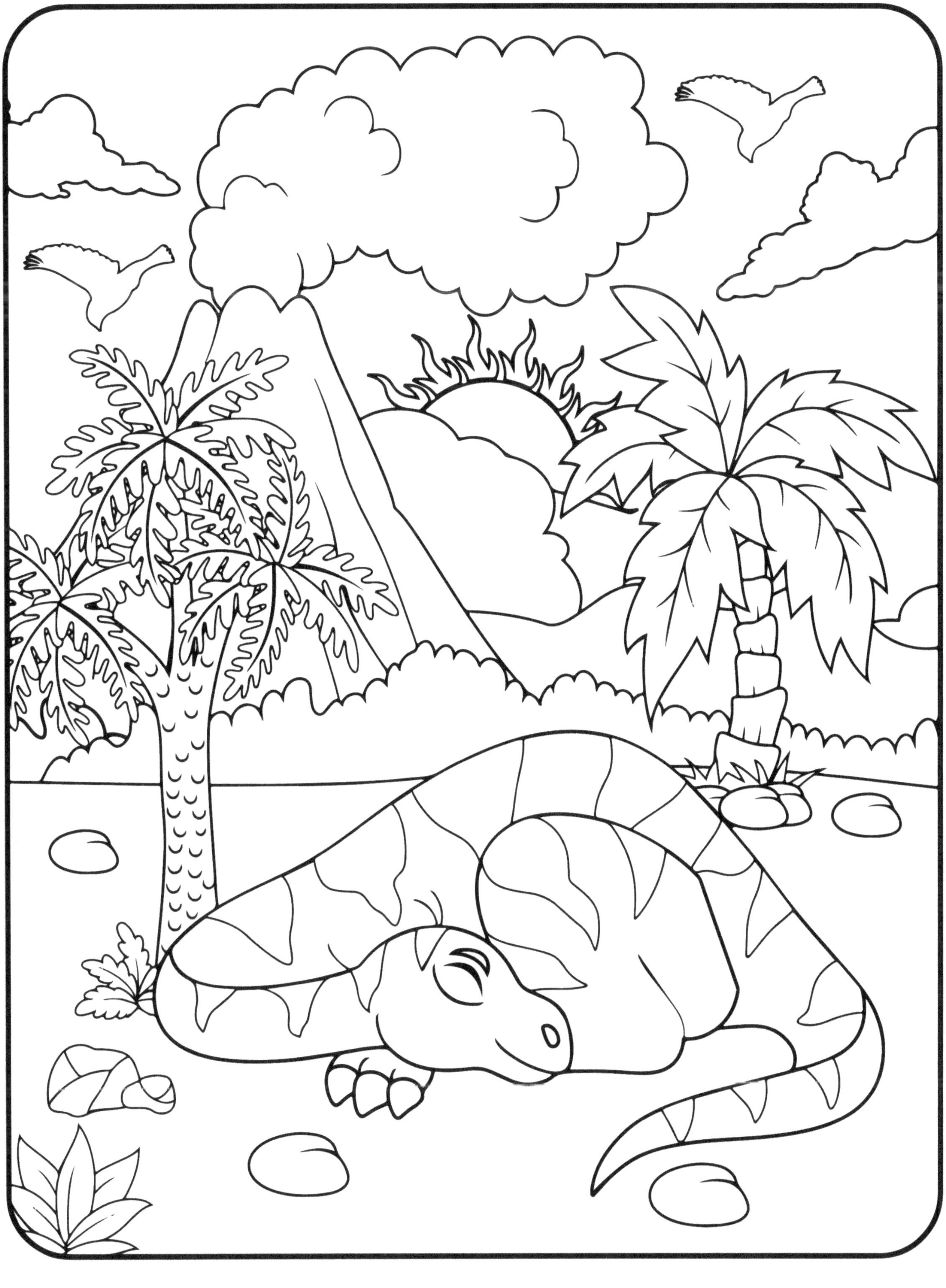

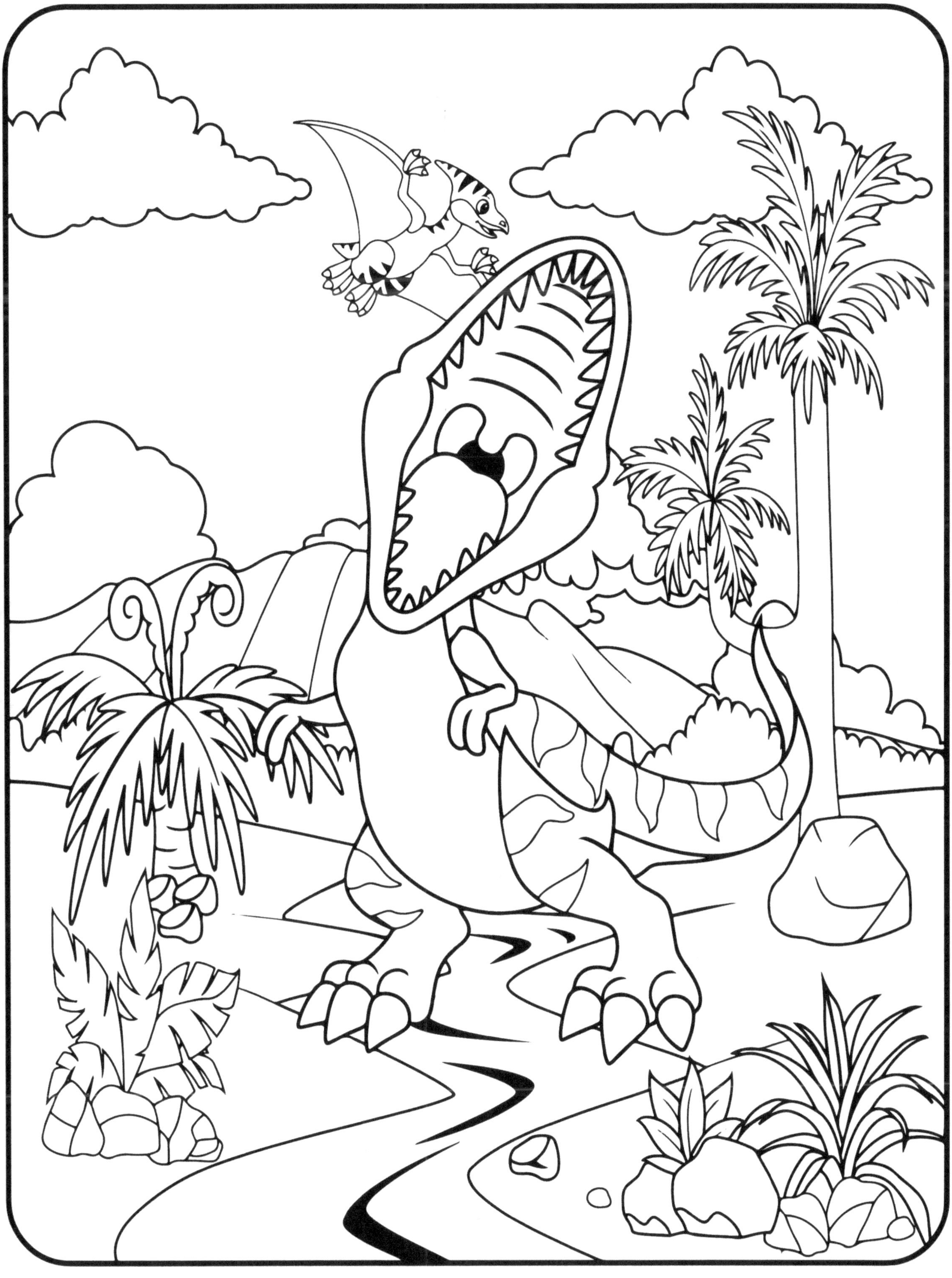

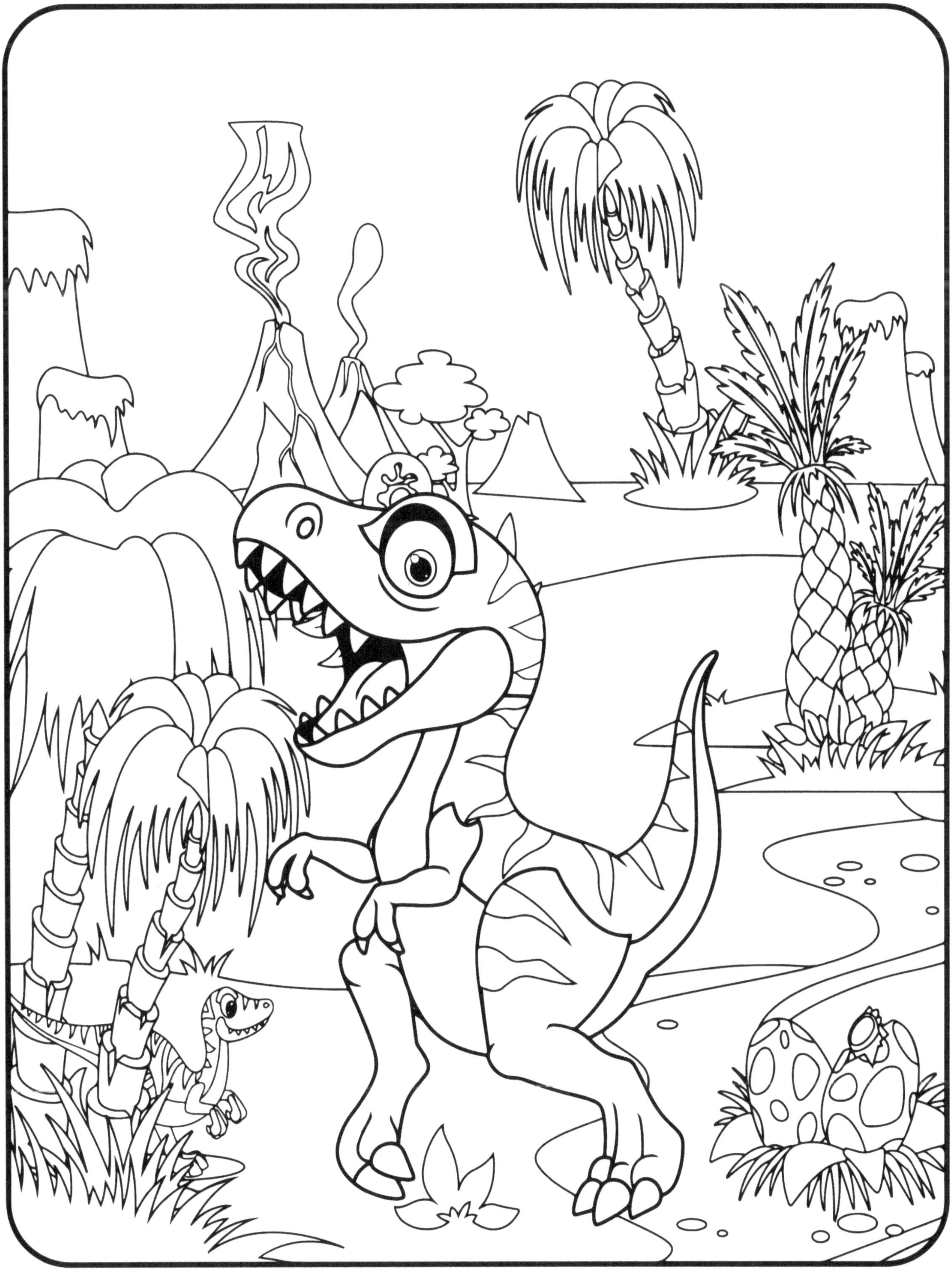

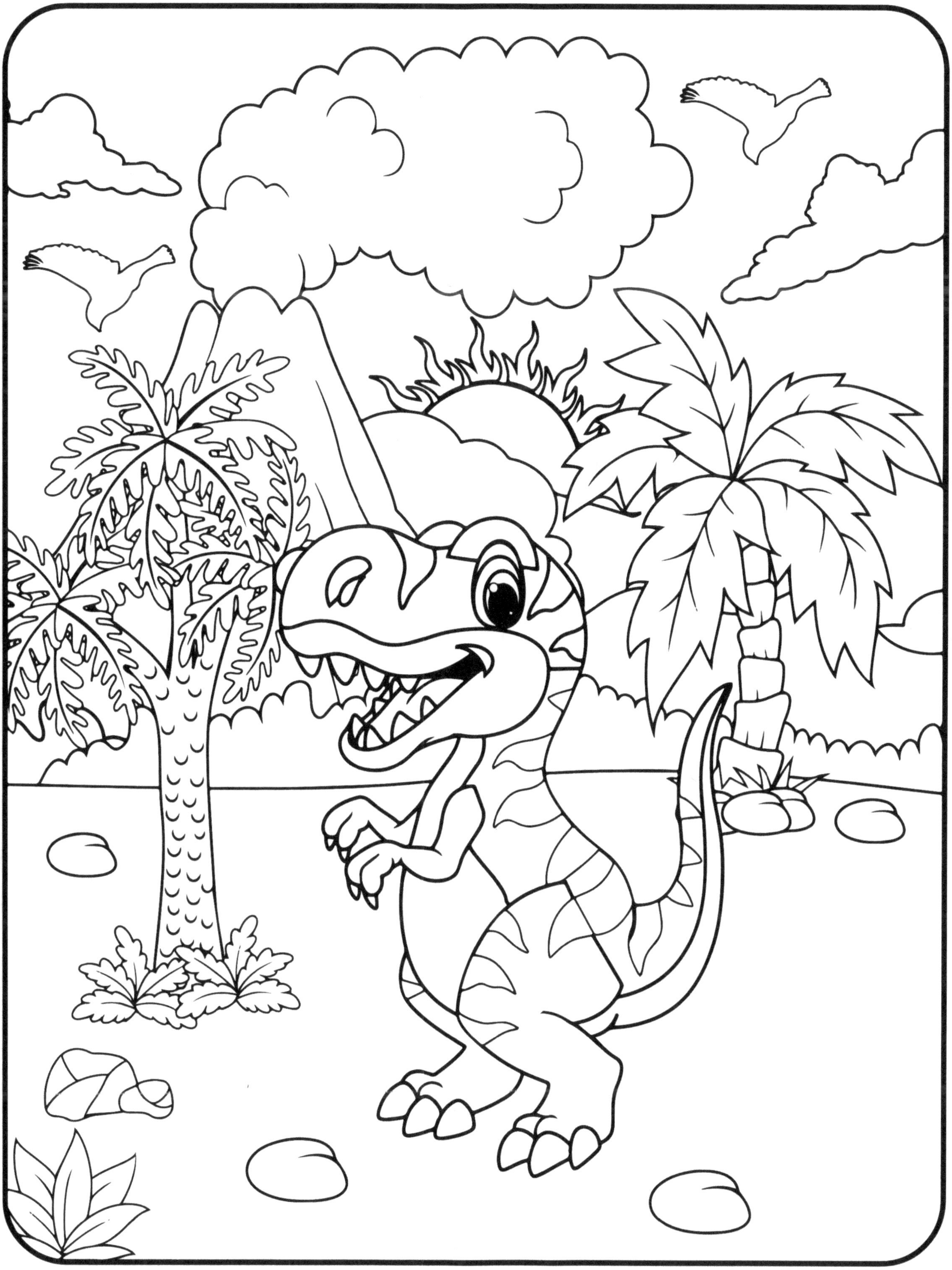

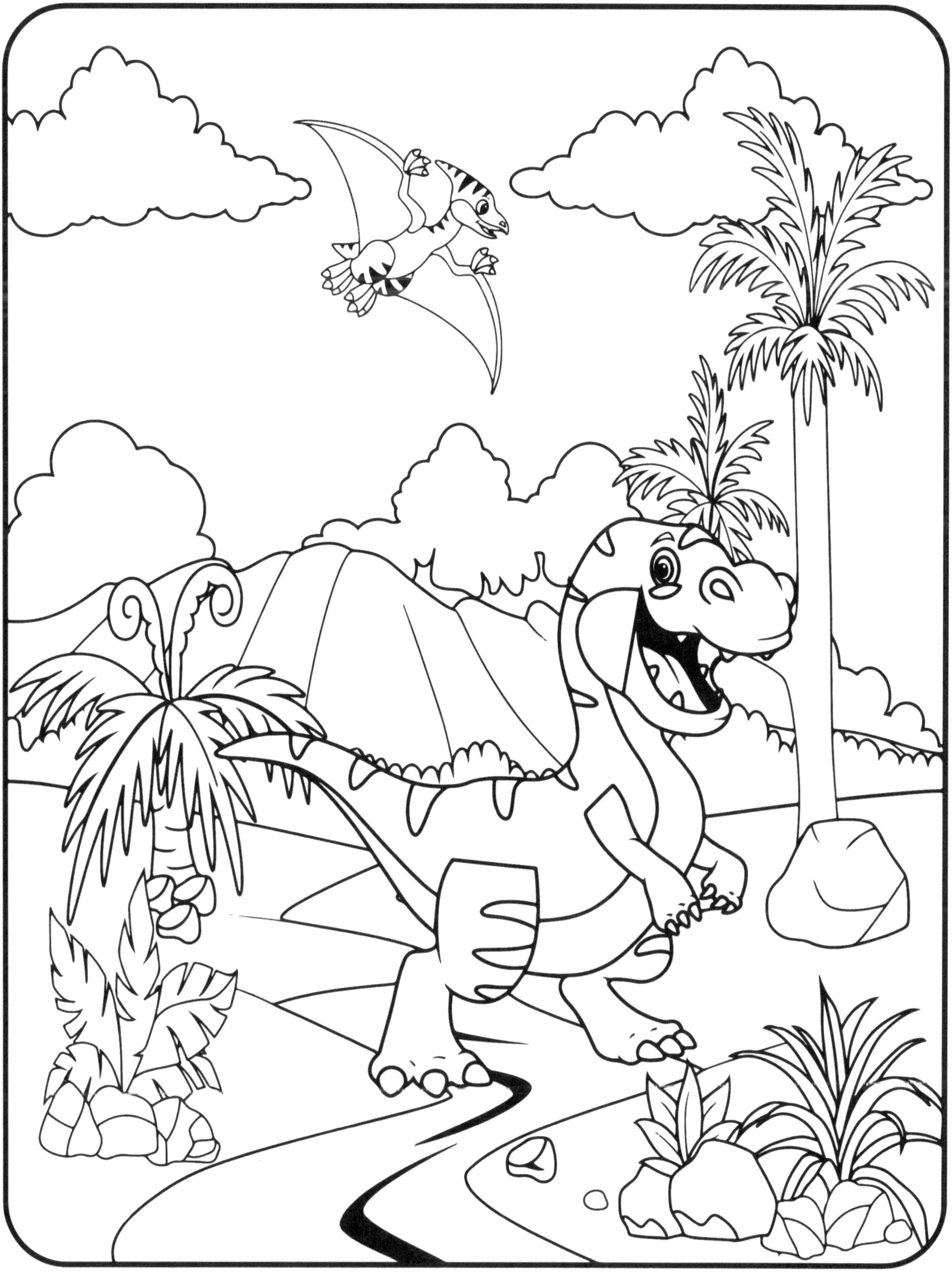

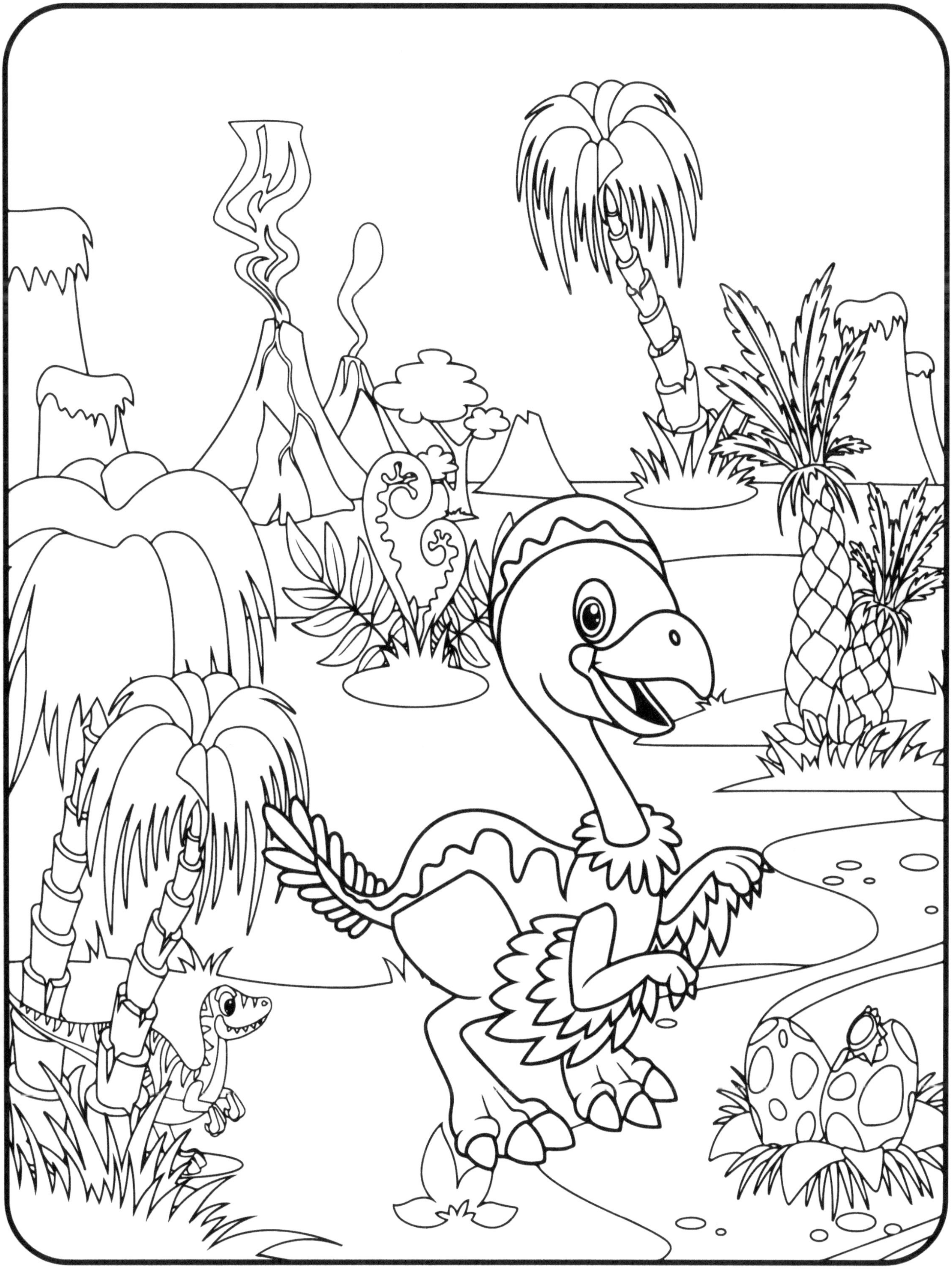

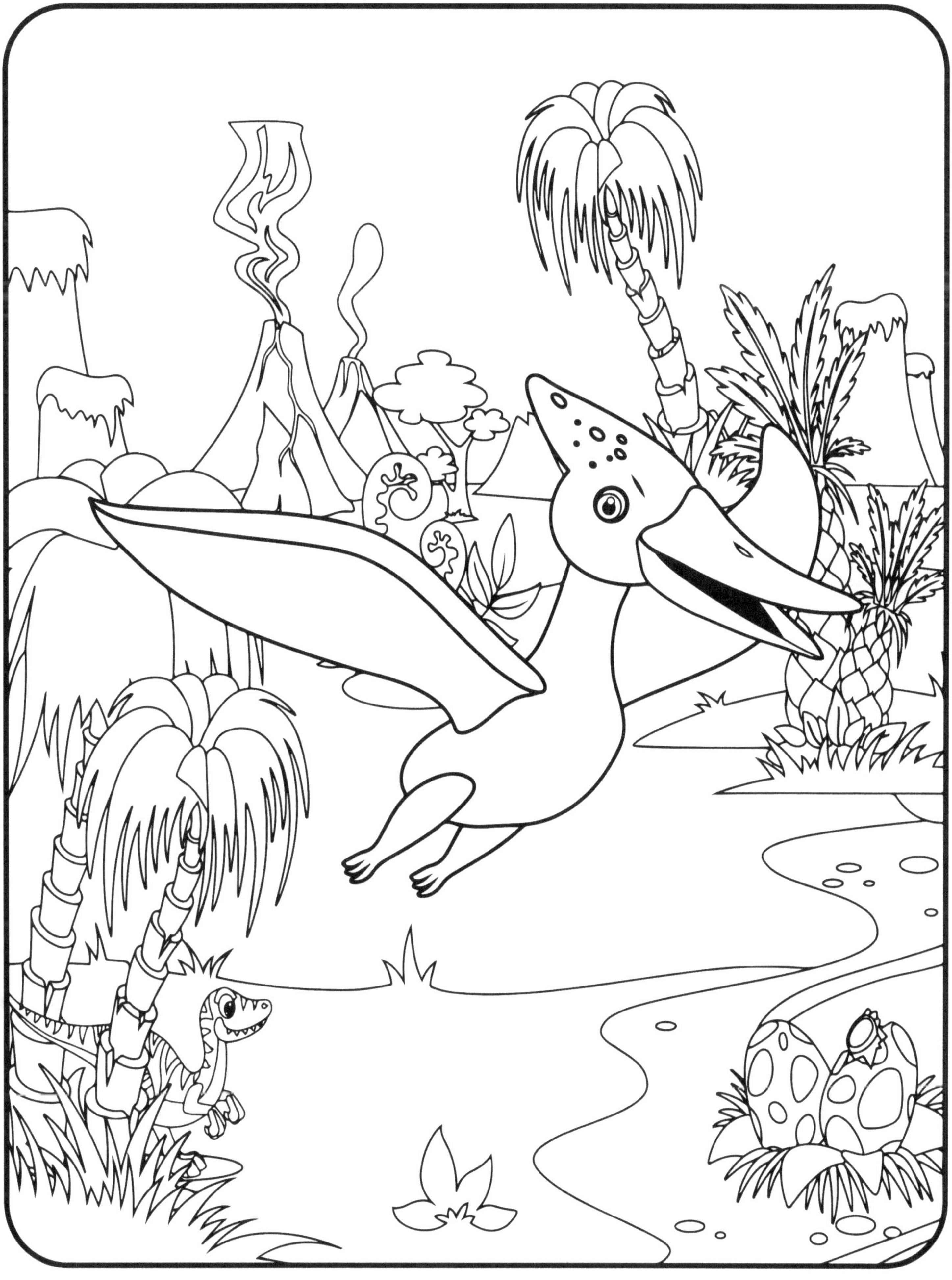

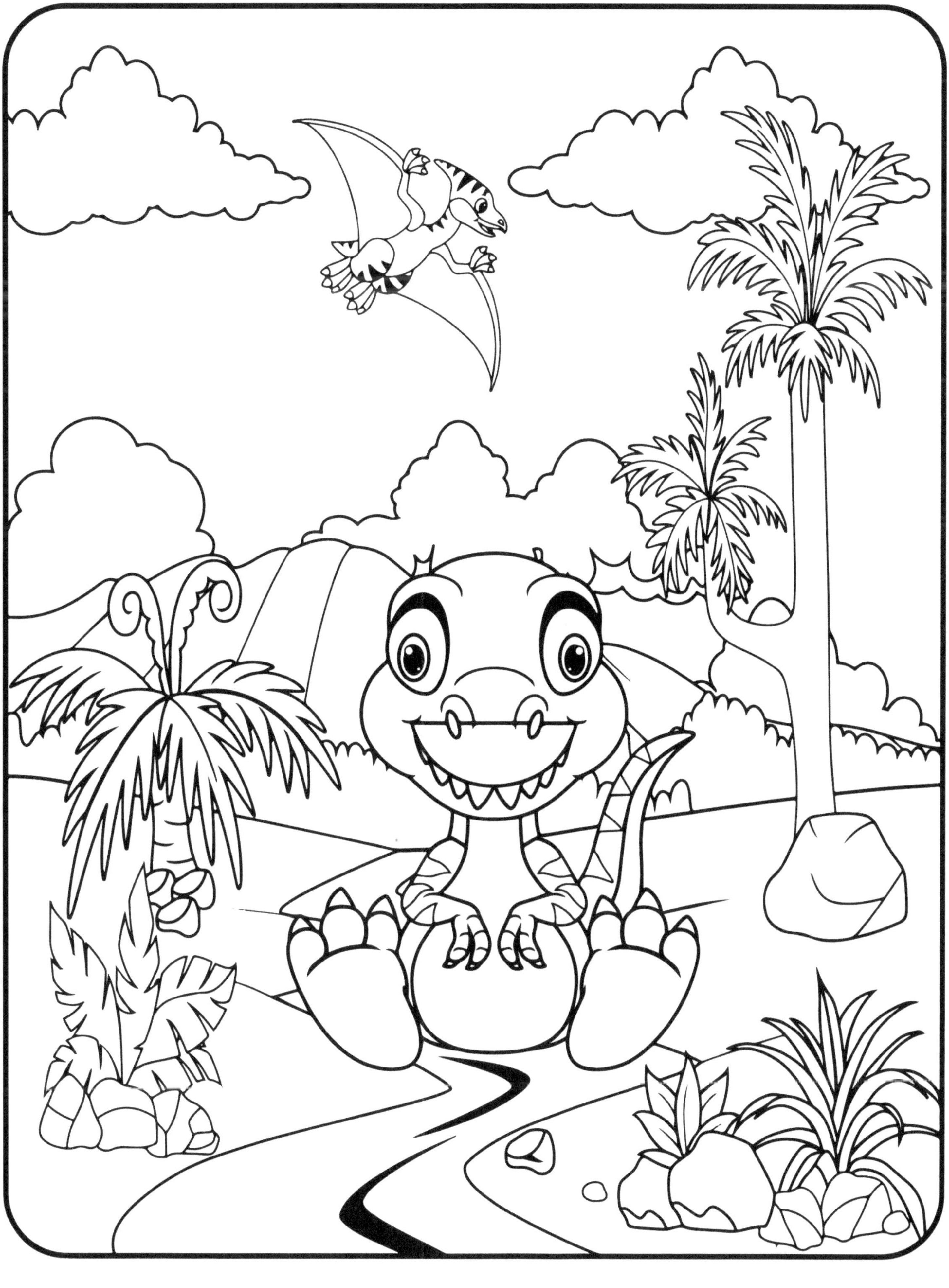

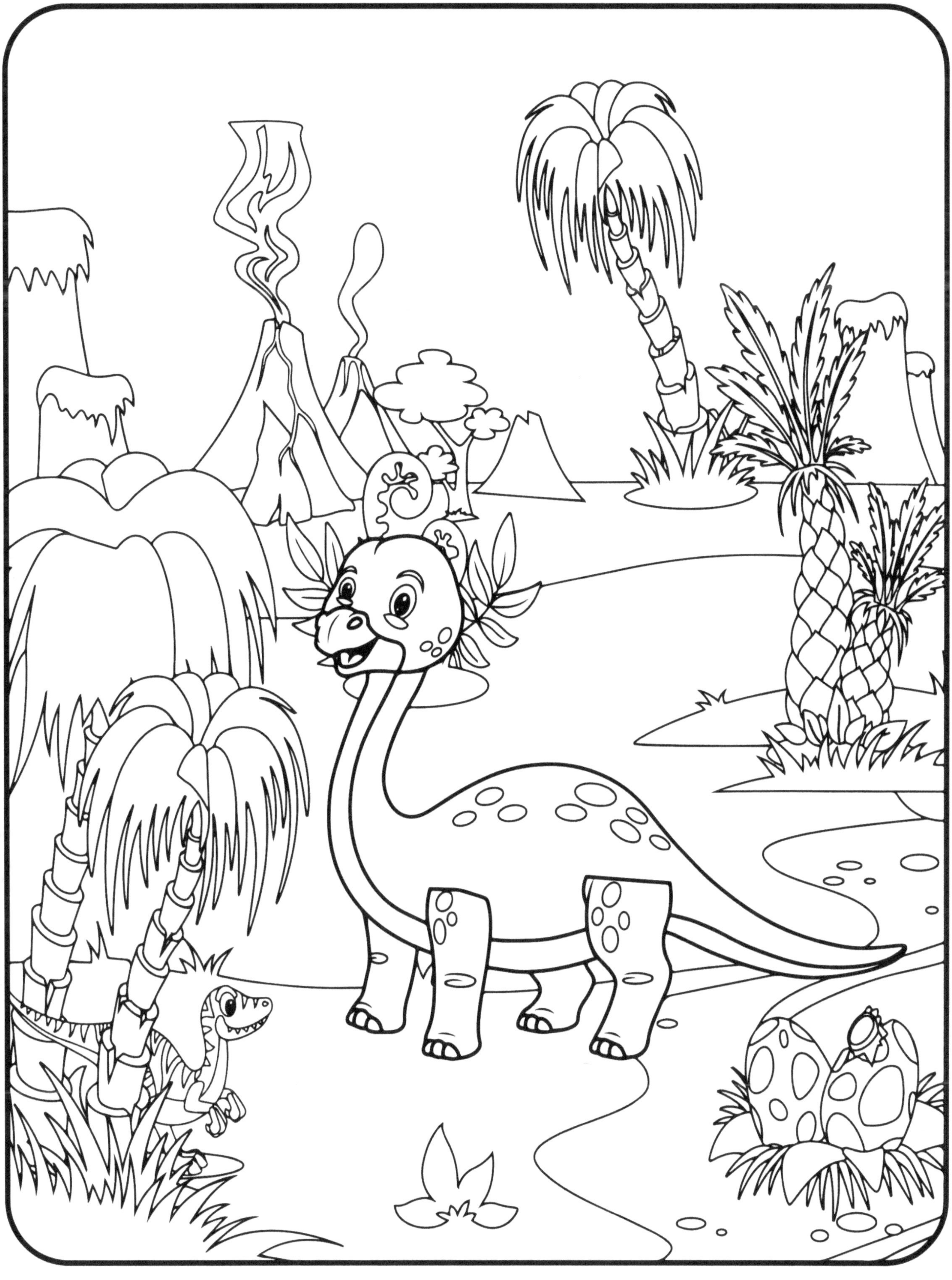

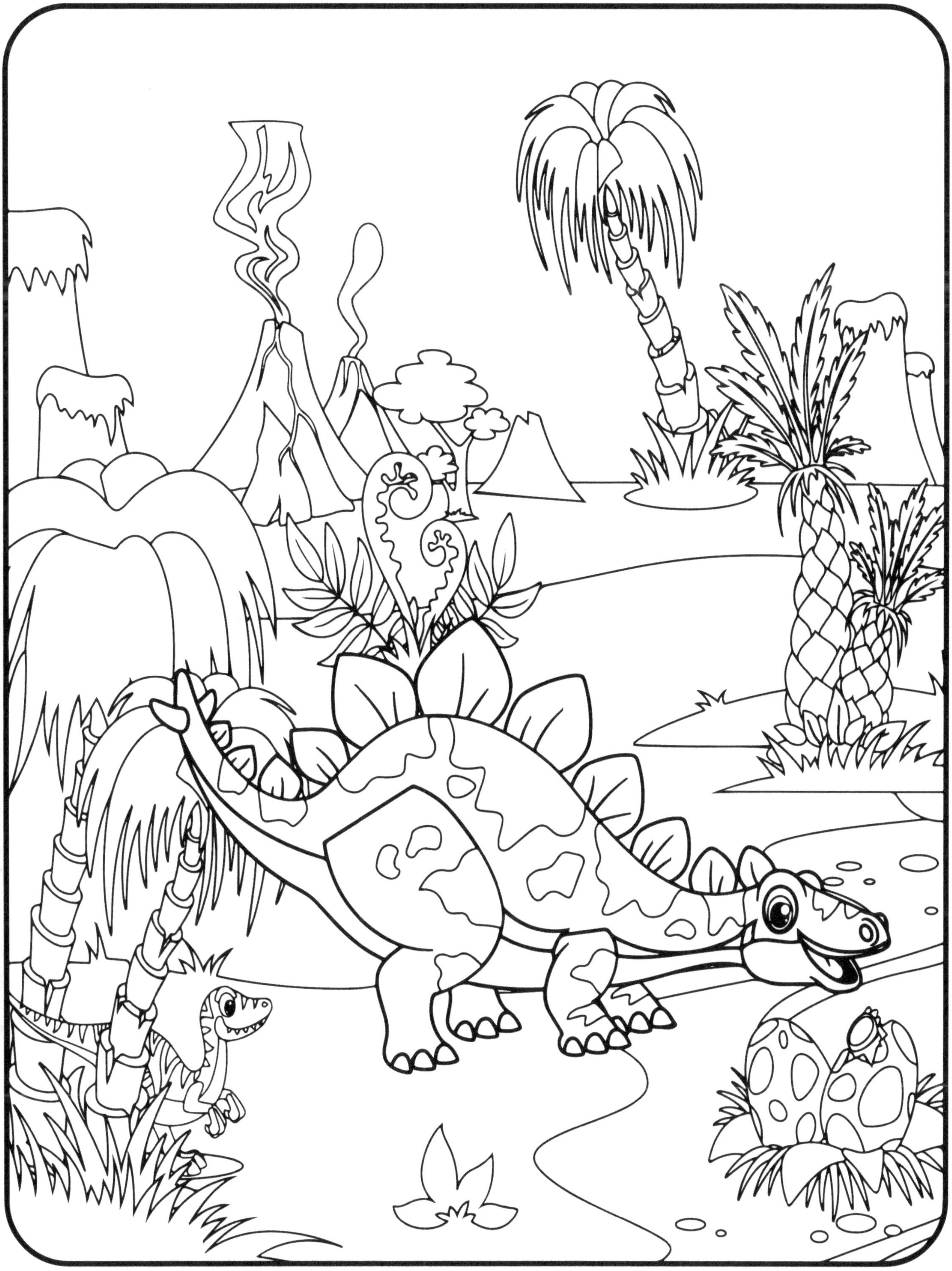

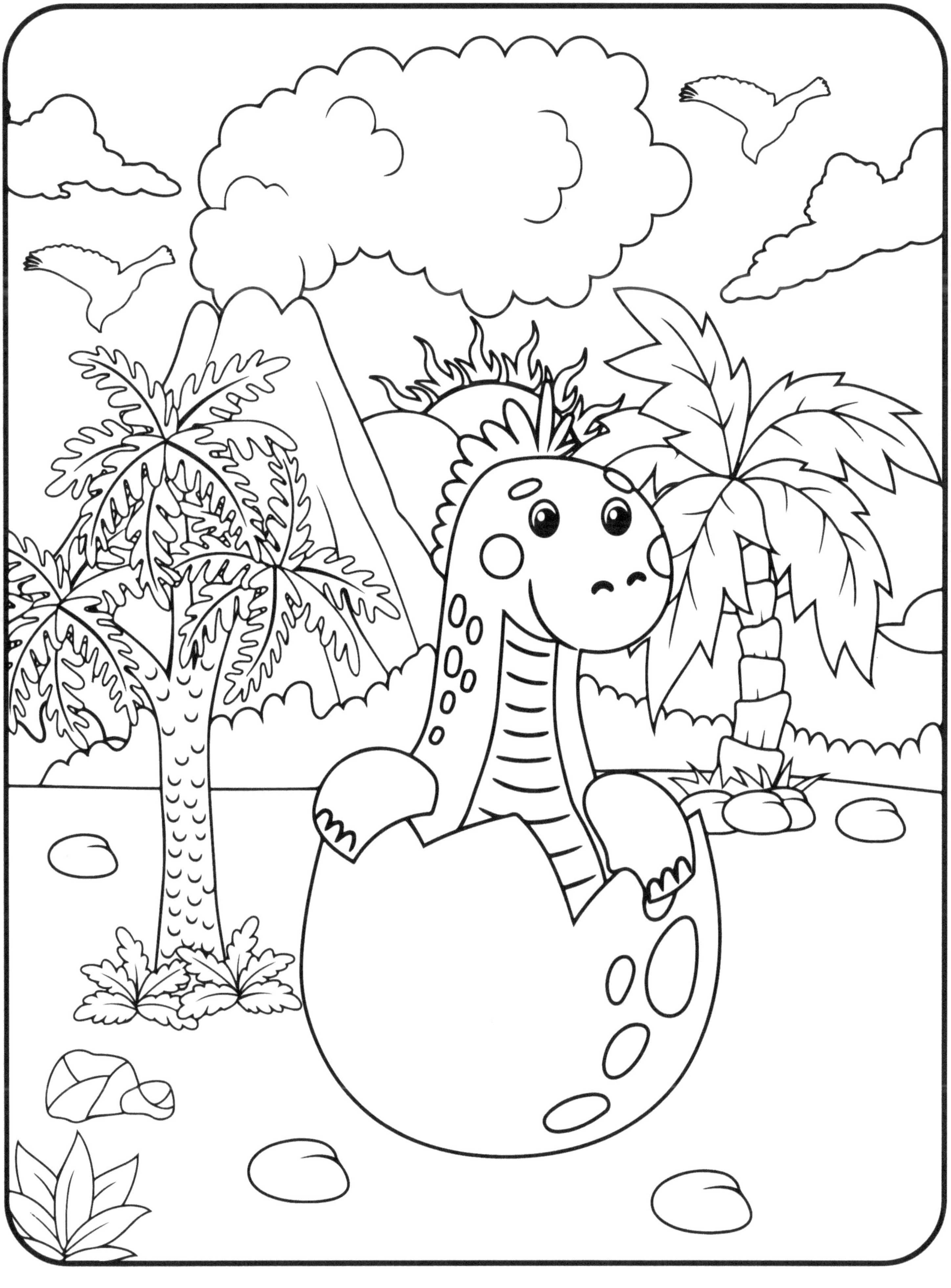

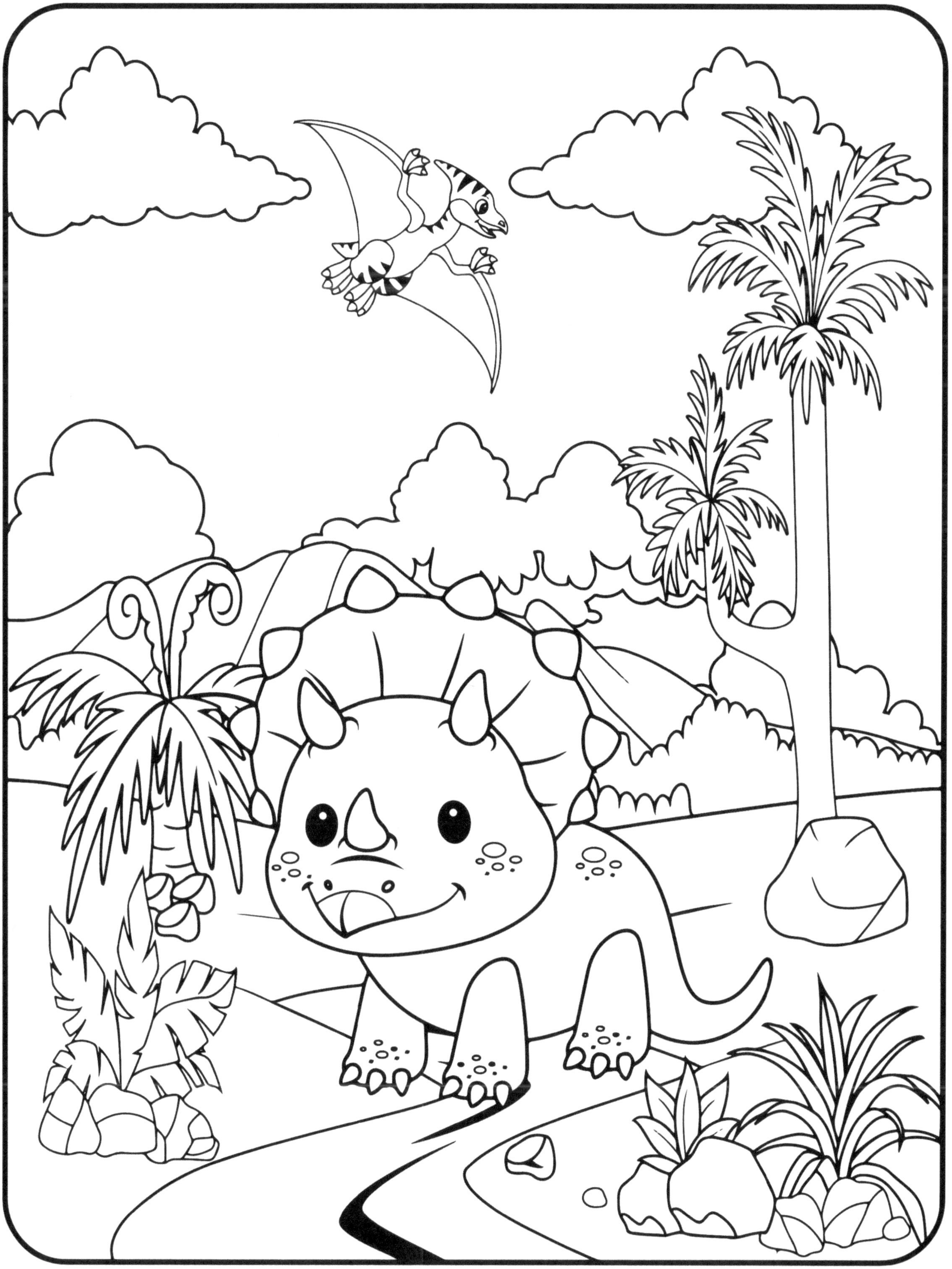

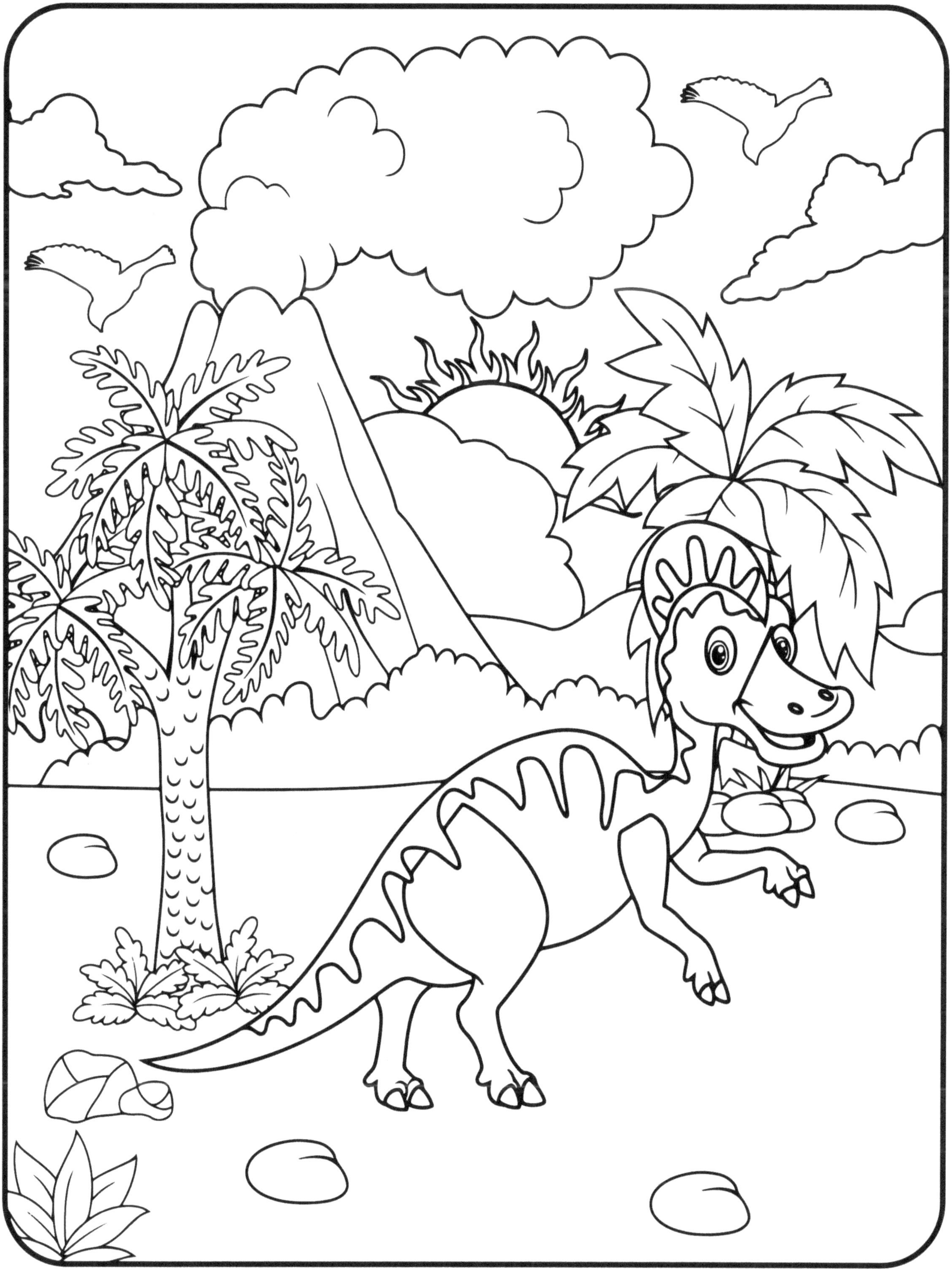

www.ingramcontent.com/pod-product-compliance
Lightning Source LLC
Chambersburg PA
CBHW082112220526
45472CB00009B/2153
* 9 7 9 8 3 2 8 6 3 3 5 3 6 *